More Adventures
of a
Mainstream
Metaphysical Mom

Other Titles by M. A. Payton

Adventures of a Mainstream Metaphysical Mom: Choosing Peace of Mind in a World of Diverse Ideas

"Soul"utions: Achieving Financial, Intellectual, Physical, Social, and Spiritual Balance with Soul

Birth Mix Patterns™: Astrology, Numerology, and Birth Order, and their Effects on the Past, Present, and Future

Birth Mix Patterns™: Astrology, Numerology, and Birth Order, and their Effects on the Families & Other Groups that Matter

Birth Mix Patterns™ and Loving Relationships using Astrology, Numerology, and Birth Order

Healing What's Real: Expanding Your Personal Power with Mind Over Matter Techniques

More Adventures of a Mainstream Metaphysical Mom

Finding Peace While Raising Teens, Building a Community, and Consciously Following-Through

M. A. Payton

Author of *Healing What's Real,*
Birth Mix Patterns and *"Soul"utions.*

The Left Side
Asheville, North Carolina

Interior body text is set in 12 point Centar by Pete Masterson, Æonix
Publishing Group, www.aeonix.com
Cover photo by Debbie Johnson Photogrpahy,
www.debbiejohnsonphotography.com
Editing by Michele Caprario, APen2Paper@aol.com

ISBN: 978-0-9719804-6-4
LCCN: 2010916799

Published by
The Left Side
1354 Heathbrook Circle
Asheville, North Carolina 28803

Phone: 828-681-1728
www.MichellePayton.com

Printed in the United States of America

What professionals are saying about Michelle Payton's work:

"I so appreciated Michelle coming onto 'The Way of the Toddler Hour.' Not only was she an insightful and knowledgeable guest, but she offered both me and my listeners tools that have begun to make a difference in my life already! ...She is, indeed, one of my all-time modern day meta-physical mothering heroines!"   —Leta Hamilton, Seattle, WA Area, Author & Presenter, www.thewayofthetoddler.com

"As a radio host and mother, I am encouraged by the special work Michelle is doing through her books and teachings which embrace the "special gifts" all children are born with and want to preserve into their adulthood."
—Jillian Mass Backman, I.T.'S For You, 96.4 FM, WI/Chicago Area, www.wlkg.com, www.jillianmaasbackman.com

"Michelle Payton has proven to us that you can still have fun and be a Mainstream Metaphysical Mom!"   —"Girls Just Wanna Have Fun" with Kelly & Amber, CA

Readers of Adventures of a Mainstream Metaphysical Mom (Book One) have said:

"I couldn't put your book down! I read it from cover to cover in two days!"

"I have had the pleasure to read two of your books, *Adventures of a Meta-physical Mom* and *"Soul"utions*. Both of which I enjoyed immensely. I found it comforting to find that I am not alone in the challenges often faced when stepping 'out of the box' to make my dreams a reality."

"It's about time this type of book is available."

"Let me preface this e-mail by telling you that I have NEVER written to ANY author after having read their book. This is the first time that I have most gladly been moved to do so... I feel much more comfortable on the path that I have chosen due to much of the things that you wrote. I thank you for putting your thoughts down on paper for me to read."

Acknowledgements

Thanks to my children—Leslie, Alex and Emma—for the endless writing material. Thanks to my husband, Karl, for being my partner on every level. I love and appreciate you all!

Contents

Table of Quotations

I. Introduction

40-Something Aches and Pains, Enlightenment and Consciousness

A jug fills drop by drop. — Buddha

I began writing the first *Adventures of a Mainstream Metaphysical Mom* when my oldest daughter was around 8-years-old. Her brother trails behind her by two years, and their baby sister is 8 years younger than our boy (this is the Universe's way of giving me a break between puberty chaoses). For those who have ever parented, grand parented, aunted, uncled, mentored, or just regularly observed parenting of youngsters ages 9+, you are aware of the interaction that takes place with these "beings" as they take a new shape, and another, and another. Initially, the double-digit age (10+) has been a major landmark for each of our kids. "I'm no longer one digit, I'm now two digits."

But the "Do this because I'm your mom and I say so" position loses its authoritative zing as they get older. And when they hit an even riper age, it is accompanied by a string of responses containing or insinuating "why?"

along with "I don't have to because I am older, smarter and know better than mom." Or, better yet, if forced to do as they are told, in return I get the "You're ruining my life!" spiel. The best way to summarize this (for me) is "UGH." I mean, come on, can't I just drift along in my mainstream metaphysical bliss of everything happens for a reason and continuous enlightenment? One minute I have my eyes closed with relaxed palms up receiving the divine and then my eyes pop open looking over my shoulder as one of my kids demands my attention. Really?

There is another awareness that has developed being 40+ and simultaneously a parent of college, high school and elementary aged children that has surprised me. Being the intuitive parent that I am (and we all are), I could see that as my kids got older their emotions and problems increased in intensity. In my own home, it's been important for me to find new avenues of psychic protection while still problem-solving as a mother.

My kids are also becoming (or are) taller, physically stronger, and are in many ways smarter and faster than I am now. Their agile young bodies perform many tasks that I also took for granted at that stage of my life. When I forget that my 40 something body doesn't move as quickly (especially if I'm emotionally drained), there is a physical price to pay later when I do it anyway. So I'm conscious of a newly-formed caution of how I push (or not) my physical form and emotional state. As I close in on the half-way point in this temple, I am being very strategic as to how to effectively and gracefully move through this life.

As I accumulate more years, I am becoming a looooonnnnng run-on sentence. I question:

- My role as a parent and how much should be about me and about them
- Consumerism and the part that I've played (and I want to redefine more than I ever have before)

- How I can increase my independence from outside energy resources
- How my children can flourish in their own lives when they are my age, and how my husband and I can be independent at a ripe age
- How we can get our kids through school and, ideally, college (monetarily and motivationally) so that they can become productive, contributing adults
- How I can connect more with personal and professional communities outside of (those connected to) my children as I become an empty nester
- What I should study (as a lifelong student), offer and expand personally and professionally with this newly-found time on my hands
- How I handle (my older children's) potential life partners as they introduce new relationships into the family mix
- How I can best help my family through even more change as I expand my soul community (including a move to Asheville, North Carolina)

But wait, there's more. Always more.

In this book, you'll see thoughts that revolve around seeking conscious enlightenment and

- Raising a Family
- Building a Community
- Achieving Health
- Following-Through

As I share my thoughts, some reading this will say, "Michelle, you made a bad decision and I would never do that." OK, so, do better. Others may say, "Oh, you are as human as I am." Or even better, "You think that's bad, well I did such and such." So take my mainstream and metaphysical momness, friendness, sisterness, auntness, passer-byerness, good Samaritanness, 40+ness path work and observances however you see fit. But I will say that even if you completely disagree with everything I say in this book (and you will on some fronts) then you have learned something about yourself, because you can only know "sweet" if you know "sour."

For me, it's helpful when someone bellies up on the hard and even soft and subtle subjects. I was in a local Chinese restaurant one day for lunch and the owner said, "Michelle, I read your book *Adventures of a Mainstream Metaphysical Mom* (book 1). My husband can't believe that you would share so much of yourself to the world." It must be some karmic thing. Maybe I was a triple secret agent in a past life and now it's time for me to tell all. My kids would call this "TMI" or Too Much Information. So while it is likely that you will both resonate with or judge within moments of reading any given section, such is the result of reading about the life of someone who can't help writing her truth at the moment.

II. Raising a Family and Conscious Thinking

To enjoy good health, to bring true happiness to one's family, to bring peace to all, one must first discipline and control one's own mind. If a man can control his mind he can find the way to enlightenment, and all wisdom and virtue will naturally come to him.

—Buddha

In my book *Birth Mix Patterns: Astrology, Numerology and Birth Order for Families and Other Groups that Matter*, I analyzed dark leaders and drew a parity between their lack of positive direction and similarities to troubled teens in America. In *Mainstream Metaphysical Mom* style, I talk about my experiences with my children, how I apply my mainstream and metaphysical training to ease through the various transitions (not always easy), and questions about how you might apply the learning in your life as a parent, aunt or uncle, grandparent, mentor to others, and/or kind and compassionate adult.

Teens are tough, and the siblings that follow behind them wanting to emulate them are even more challenging. I look at my life and say, "I'm glad I'm a mom." In the same breath I say, "I'll be so happy when they are 25 and older." In this section I'll talk about brain physiology, my theories on why teenagers lie, suggestions on how we can move past the deception—sometimes with grace and sometimes clumsily, and how we can apply mind over matter tools to allow time to heal all wounds.

A radio host said to me during an interview, you seem to contradict yourself in various books. I proudly announced, "Absolutely!" Why is this a good thing? Because I'm very aware that I'm not the same person I was the day, hour or minute before my last experience. I will also say in the same breath that every move I've made was supposed to happen.

For instance, in my first *Mainstream Metaphysical Mom* book when my kids were in elementary school or younger, I took offense to an adult that advised me that you have to be careful who your kids hang out with. They may develop "reputations." "What?" I said! It's part of my kids' job descriptions to lend helping hands!"

But as my kids became young adults, things got tougher. I was no longer in parent Nirvana where you could pick up the phone and call another parent and say, "Suzy pushed my little girl off the swing at school." Each child is different, so I was unprepared in many ways, each time one of my children moved into "teendom." Let's talk about that first.

Physiology of a Teenage Brain—Not Fully Developed until 25?! How much can I take?

Always aim at complete harmony of thought and word and deed. Always aim at purifying your thoughts and everything will be well. —Mohandas Gandhi

A 3-year-old's brain is twice as active as an adult's brain with lots of little wires (much more than a normal adult ends up with), but they aren't set in patterns yet.

For a visual, imagine a wig of long, straight hair. Look at the many fine strands. Then imagine making many small, tight braids in the hair. Notice that the strands are now thicker as braids. The original long, straight hair is similar to the many strands of an infant brain, and the braided hair is a teenage and older brain (fewer loose strands).

Our young people are having many new experiences and are not being stifled as much by repetitive patterns and adult rules. This puts them in a type of exploratory cosmic trance state. By age 11-12 many connections are dropped (called pruning) to create a more powerful and efficient brain. By teenage years—these post children, pre-adults—spend more time reasoning vs. exploring, and laboring to think through situations to define what's right and wrong. So while brain cells are formed by this time, connections and patterns of wiring in the cells develop over time and mature by about age 25. The result is our adult brain has thicker wires with more programmed patterns and is more about visualizing and imagery (remembering in a sense) to get the answers of right or wrong because we have more experiences to pull from.

Knowing more about the physiology of the brain, does that change your mind about infants to age 25? Why? What do we do with that as parents, relatives, mentors or professionals that deal with children and developing teens daily?

Believing in "God"

Each one prays to God according to his own light.

—Mohandas Gandhi

While we have developing brains, we also have developing traditions. I have a teenage wannabe (our third born). (She looks up to siblings that are 8 and 10 years older than her.) At the time of writing this chapter, she was about 7-years-old and a very social, only child, intuitive Pisces and master number Life Path 11.

My husband once asked, "Why is our grocery bill so high?" One of the primary contributors is feeding dozens of other elementary and high school kids within a 5-mile radius. Frankly, I love this. To be permitted to listen in on these kids' thoughts was just a hoot and this day was no different.

My youngest was sitting down for dinner with her little friend and she asked, "What is the prayer that you say before dinner?" Her friend recited her dinner prayer, and my daughter began repeating it. My youngest then looked up at me and said, "Mommy, why don't we pray at dinner?" I explained to her that we have different rituals. And she turned to her friend and said, "See, I told you my mom doesn't believe in God."

We have a number of rituals, and acknowledge a number of energies in our household that our kids think of as traditions. Some may label our traditions as religion, but that doesn't quite fit the bill. My two older children started asking about more advanced "faith" based labels when they were the about same age, so with as little inflection as possible I responded, "We do believe in an energy that could be called God by other people. It's all the same, people just call God different things." I knew that she was also referring to Jesus—she hadn't yet learned how to separate the two when she was introduced to the concept in one of her Christian pre-schools. So I addressed this head on and explained, "Jesus plays a different role in our household than possibly your friends." My teenage niece happened to be standing there and said, "Well done, Aunt Michelle."

It takes time to integrate mainstream and metaphysical information in a way that is easy but safe for youngsters to repeat (and they will repeat it). Too much information too soon can create discomfort with "certain masses" and alienation could result. It wasn't a big explanation, but it was enough for the moment.

By the time my oldest went to college, she was dabbling in the idea of Christianity and a male only God (I won't even get started). My son feels more comfortable in the Earth Religion area. My husband remains more of a "Be kind and good things happen" kind of guy. Over time, being married to the *mainstream metaphysical mom,* he enjoys gathering information (7 analyzer and seeker of truth in his numerology), and one of his hobbies has become researching traditions, religions and their intentions.

We have a lovely eclectic and open-minded extended family for the most part. And when my husband's brother and his wife asked if my husband and I would be their first born's (more traditional title) godparents, we were extremely honored. The day before the baptism, we met with the clergyman of the Christian church to discuss the process. Part of the tradition is to repeat certain "promises"—rededicate yourself to Jesus Christ, support the Christian church, and proclaim allegiance to the belief system. As the clergyman read more and more of the text and prayers, I had to quickly and kindly say (so the attention remained primarily on the family and not my traditions), "I'm going to have to admit that this isn't my tradition and I can't make any declarations. I respect that this is a sacred place. (Turning to my sister-in-law) And If I'm called on, I will introduce your son to this and many other streams of thought, but I don't feel comfortable lying in church." My sister-in-law said to me (and I summarize), "Why do you think we picked you? We know that you would be open-minded enough to introduce him to many ideas and allow him to make his own decision." The clergyman agreed, "You can observe in silence. This is completely acceptable in our church." Relieved, I stood in silence for the rest of the meeting and the next day at the baptism. My husband and two daughters and balance of my extended family went up for communion, while my son and I looked on. It was a warm family gathering with all standing in love.

Following the service, my mother-in-law said to me when we were alone, "I know that must have been uncomfortable for you, but thank you." Quickly thanking her and giving a "family is important" type thought, it reminded me that with certain faith masses, my children will face those with less understanding and a lack of kindness at times. The eclectic training that I provided as a parent, godparent, and eventually grand parent must include how to effectively integrate into the mainstream, while still observing out of the box traditions.

About two years after my youngest made the "God" comment, she said "Mommy, I've written you a story that I know you'll like," and then handed me a two page, handwritten, story she titled "The Budah" (her spelling). It was about a mom, dad and their daughter "Budah" doing daily life when all of a sudden an earthquake hit. She wrote "...She goes outside (and) Budah feels the ground shake again, then Budah realized it was an earthquake! ... (She) shared (the news) around the world. Everyone ran to a safe place. In (her city) Budah took everyone to a safe place (as well). But Budah didn't make it. Budah passed. When the earthquake was over everyone came out but couldn't find Budah. They knew she was dead. For her thanks, the town people made a statue..." Her story of bravery, giving of oneself, giving thanks, and (the possibility of) a young female spiritual leader were connections she finally made as a third grader.

Were you ever in an uncomfortable position because you had a less mainstream idea or practice? How can you integrate comfortably into the mainstream and still practice your traditions? Or does that matter?

Keeping the Family Fiber in Place when Lying is the Status Quo

If patience is worth anything, it must endure to the end of time.
And a living faith will last in the midst of the blackest storm.
—Mohandas Gandhi

Traditions build family fiber, and kids testing their boundaries can break them down. As I walked around minding all my kids' businesses, POW!, they played me like a fiddle to get their ways. What that means is there is a stage in their lives when they look me straight in the eyes and tell me lies. Constantly! What I've come to realize is if my kids are telling me the truth all the time (as much as it pains me), then I'm stunting their growth. Seems counterintuitive, but they have to make some mistakes on their own to get to the other side of increased ability to reason.

I don't know what wise philosopher said this, but what doesn't kill you makes you stronger! And while, frankly, having teenagers has been stressful, and a real challenge for maintaining an enlightened state, I've become a smarter, more grateful conscious living parent, guardian, aunt, and mentor every day. I continue to embrace that everything happens for a reason, and have gratitude for my experiences. But I would also add that with teenagers I'm more thankful once particular events are over. Or are they?

I was setting up at a trade show that I've gone to for over a decade and it always takes me twice as long to set up the booth because I am catching up with a number of my friends. Of course, being in the middle of thinking about and writing this book, I talked about my teenagers and wannabe teenager (in elementary school) constantly. One of my "catch up with what you've been doing for the past year" friends said, "Well this is what my teenager gave me this year." She opened up her cell phone and flashed a picture of an infant. She called it her "Prom Baby." Completing our bond, we hugged and patted each other on the backs for getting through life this far and asked the Universe for enough patience and wisdom to get our kids through high school, and envisioned their completions of college or trade school degrees.

Can we be enlightened and raise teenagers? There are days when I say "yes." And then days where I say "pretty please let the answer be yes."

My Teenagers' Protest – Everyone Lies!

Three things cannot be long hidden: the sun, the moon, and the truth.
—Buddha

When writing our adventures in this book my oldest teenager said, "Mom, we (she and her teenage brother) have been meaning to talk to you about your idea that teenagers lie. Everyone lies. Even little kids lie (like her little sister) and adults."

While my teenagers began planning their revolt I explained why the teenage phase was such a big deal. I'm not sure she really heard it, but... Little ones lie about putting their toys away. When adults lie they are of age and have to legally take responsibility for their lies (well some take responsibility and some don't, but they are still of age). When teenagers lie, adults/guardians/parents have bigger messes to clean up—teenage pregnancy and a child raising a child, illegal drug and alcohol use, driving under the influence, truancy at school, and the list goes on. While teenagers are dabbling in the adult staging area, the responsible adults and guardians have to protect themselves from the stress, anxiety, disappointment, fear, not to mention the law!

I decided to ask a handful of high school teenagers between 10th and 12th grades why they lie? This is far from quantitative, more like an anonymous focus group. So that they would share more openly and to protect their privacy, I asked them to write down their answers and they responded with answers like:

(I lie because) "They wouldn't let me do stuff otherwise."

"I do (lie) to my dad, (but not to my mom) because my mom is straightforward with me and I owe it to her to do the same."

"So they won't ground me or so I won't lose their trust and so mom and dad think I'm a good little girl."

"On occasion because I can do stuff they wouldn't normally let me do."

When I asked if their parents trusted them, they said:

"They don't know I drink, and I'm not a bad kid."

"Mostly."

"Half of them do, because I tell her the truth."

"I think so because they never caught me in a lie."

So how can parents and guardians maintain a family fiber, but still allow their teens to safely form their adult patterns? And how do we guide them through the drugs, alcohol and sex pressures?

I asked these same teens how many times per week they found themselves depressed and why. They came back with:

"Once a month." "Built-up stress from friends and school."

"Maybe two or three times (per week)." "Because of stress from school or boyfriends or because I feel like I have no friends or I'm not important or I feel bad about things that have happened in the past."

"Probably everyday for short amounts of time." "(Because of) stress, boys, life, parents, childhood, just thinking basically how I look (aka fatness)."

"Once or twice (per week)." "Missing a friend. I don't know."

So how and when do we give our aspiring adults room to grow, experiment and step out of parental controls?

Sometimes it's the "Shoot First and Ask Questions Later" Parenting Style

Chaos is inherent in all compounded things. Strive on with dili-gence. —Buddha

I had just been to high school with my son to talk to his counselor and select teachers because he had been skipping school. He had two and a half semesters left and I really didn't know how much more I could handle.

When meeting with the counselor, I was going to take him out of the high school and put him in (what's called in our area) middle college. This meant he would take the balance of his courses at a community college with no authority to come on the high school campus his senior year. He had the intellect (3.5+ cumulative grade point and strong SAT scores), but high school rules (like having to ask to go to the bathroom or not being permitted to use his cell phone) and the more dramatic student population didn't bring out the best in him.

However after so many incidences, it became a good thing to shoot first and ask questions later. For me, shoot first meant I was getting intuitive jabs that activated "mom protection mode." It was less important to know what was going on than it was to pull my son out of the way of the feeling of upcoming negativity. It kept my teens ever so slightly afraid of what I would do, because I wasn't always predictable. My son had an uncanny way of finding out how the rules worked and then finding loopholes to manipulate situations. But he could never 100% quite figure out what he was going to get from me, so loopholes were harder to find.

Some for instances, when he didn't come home until 4:30 in the morning one time, I texted every single friend he had in North Carolina looking for him. Another time the school called and said, "Michelle, your son just left campus unauthorized." I immediately texted him and said that I was going to report our vehicle stolen and the police would be looking for him immediately if he didn't get back in the school building." At first he said that a couple of his friends took my van off school premises (he gave them the key) and he was covering for them so I told him I would consider pressing charges against his friends. He had to come clean (especially since his escape was recorded on the school security video). I was basically scaring him and anyone connected to him straight.

I will also say that my son thought he was a bit of a "Bad Ass" or "BA" for short. When we moved to Asheville, while the schools were very good, he put on the "BA" façade and attracted that. He got in some trouble but he could have gotten in really deep if we weren't watching and striking quickly enough.

What was important to know was what do teens want? Our son's "wants" were:

- A vehicle to drive
- A cell phone
- To participate in the half day in high school and half day in college program
- To have a few dollars in his pocket (he had a job after school that he enjoyed)
- To get a college degree and for us to pay for as much of his college costs as possible

The delicate balance was to have the strength to take these things away and know when to reward him for improvement. I gathered a team of co-parents. I met with several administrators, emailed teachers regularly, and he was checking in every couple of weeks with his school counselor to give her a status report. I kept them all in the know on his punishments and my commitment to "encourage him" to succeed.

But what if you don't have cars, cell phones, and college funds as carrots to keep teens in line? School officials and teachers can truly be your friends and co-parents. They can also help you find incentives (not just punishments). There can be a lot of time invested but the payout for your teens will be unlimited. I will say that I have asked myself as my kids move into adulthood, what did we do to create such an attitude of entitlement from our kids?

Having Fun while Being Accountable –
Where's the Balance?

If you can, help others; if you cannot do that, at least do not harm them
—*Dalai Lama*

We (my husband and I) invested a lot of time being parents and had to become conscious of the fact that we trained our children to be the centers of the Universe. Hear me out.

As babies, children, teenagers and even beyond, when they need help we respond and provide. Then there comes a time, however, when they expect to be provided for while they spread their wings whether we agree on the destination or not. Are there really any cookie cutter rules for parents/guardians on when and how we cut the cord?

There are lots of opinions. Certainly Dr. Phil has a theory, and I surmise has written a book or two on the subject. And if we follow his ten clear-cut steps we will be amazing parents. In nature it seems to be pretty finite. Momma birds kick the chicks out of the nests, and they fly or not. No turning back.

When children are little they dress up in mom and dad's clothes, dress up as princesses and super heroes, role play with dolls and action figures. This is all for the sake of growing up. And when they begin to physically develop as adults, a part of them becomes confused. Where do they fit? Which doll or figure are they? How much can be fun and games, and how much requires being serious and focused? How much do they believe in their parents and extended family (using them as role models)? And when do they no longer become the centers of the Universe?

Up until my oldest was about 11, her friends would call and ask if she could "play." It became less cool to call what they were doing "play" at about 12-years-old. Preteen friends then called consciously asking if my daughter was "available." By the time she was a senior in high school, a few of her closer friends had lightened up a bit, could laugh at themselves and went back to saying "let's make a play date." Language is so interesting and important. Listen for it and it clues you in to their's and their friends' states of minds.

Adult transitions vary and we can easily lose track of when, why, how and even if they occur as parents, guardians and mentors. One of my extended family members had been staying with us on and off for about two months. She was permitted to do this because she was following the rules at her mom's house and it was a reward in her eyes. She was 16 at the time, and made friends wherever she would go. She was playing music (guitar her specialty) at our local coffee house within a week of visiting, and had a social calendar in the area in no time.

She bent a couple of our rules, and the threat of bending too hard was that she would not be permitted to visit without her mom indefinitely. So I gave her "the talk" about boundaries and staying within certain rules that would always create success for her. I gave her examples like: When driving a car there are certain rules you have to follow to keep your license; when going to school and following certain rules you obtain a degree; when paying certain bills you can have running water and electric. Putting it in her terms, you can get what you want (payment), when playing by certain rules to some extent. This was a tough concept for her to grasp, and she ultimately remained in "play" mode entering into adulthood—no high school degree, moving from place to place, not holding down a job (while her other siblings achieved the opposite). There was no when, why, or how. It was a very large "if."

When, how and why do we let go as parents, guardians, and mentors? Is drifting OK? Does it matter if we don't think it's OK?

Have you ever been at the end of your Relationship Rope?

The hunger for love is much more difficult to remove than the hunger for bread. —Mother Teresa

There's a denial that enters my reality when I am at the end of my rope, especially since I'm a mind over matter holistic healer. Aren't we always supposed to be at the top of our games and clear-headed so we can help others?

Well, as it turns out, the way I've helped others is by walking through similar fires. While I'm in a 28-year relationship, I have lived through divorce with my parents. While I have a healthy lifestyle today, my father was a chain smoker, drinker, drug user, abuser mentally and physically, and was also diagnosed "borderline schizophrenic." While I have not had the problem of being overweight, I have had the problem of being underweight. While my body is in sound working order, I have an extreme case of scoliosis. While I am educated, I am (along with my siblings) the first generation in my family to receive a college degree.

Numerous clients' have come to me because they connected to my past and see a person that has found tools to live a functional and happy life. But it isn't always functional—especially when having children—and even more challenging when they become teenagers. My second born had been suspended from school, got caught on tape for skipping school, came home smelling of "substances," his grades dropped, and he hung out with a less supervised crowd of kids. As I continued to jump in to save him from further suspension, time-activating his homework weekly, keeping contact with teachers, counselors and school administrators, I found my libido dropped, my appetite lowered, my attraction to my husband dwindled, and I felt depressed and angry regularly.

Part of my anger was that I knew the stress and unhappiness decreased my quality of life and shortened my lifespan. I would have never guessed that my third grader was easier to care for than my 17-year-old. Following my son being videotaped driving off his high school campus to skip school, I was tapped out. Unfortunately, there was more to come.

I came up with a menu of options for my son that ranged from putting him in another school, to having him graduate early (since he had enough credit hours). I limited his cell phone usage and driving privileges. If I gave him his cell phone, I monitored his texts and calls so that he was no longer communicating to people during classroom hours. And on and on and on.

And then I had my third grader that, like my two older children, thrived when seeing me in her classroom and school as a volunteer. I noticed a direct correlation with all three of my children on better behavior and grades when they saw me in school. I was burned out but wondered, "Why should my elementary school child suffer because my teenager lacked good judgment?"

In addition to my professional work and maintaining a level of personal care, this took a lot of time. My husband said, "You should volunteer less, and let me pick up some of the slack on our son's behavior issues." But he traveled weekly and couldn't consistently tend to issues and school events in the moment. I warned my husband that I was at a breaking point, but what I didn't realize is I had put my marriage on hold. Did I catch it in time?

My acid test for romantic relationship is, "How would I feel if I saw my partner in a separate romantic relationship?" I also asked as a mother, "How would I feel if my children were being raised with single or step parents (which has become more the norm)? And how would that affect their lives?" Keeping the family together was top priority. My husband was still my best friend, but the romantic part of our relationship had come undone and was a lower priority.

My romantic relationship priorities had to be reformed, refocused and of equal importance. All balls had to be in the air to get my son out of high school with high enough grades to get into college, find my way back to being involved with my husband, and enjoying a professional life and some independent activities. I also had to be keenly aware that with the Leo in me, there were certain things I had to do for myself to keep my level of joy from being completely drained. For many months, my days were being ruled by whether or not my son had a good day — i.e., he went to school, he wasn't in trouble, he was home by curfew, he was clearheaded, he was with kids with sound judgment.

Soon after my priorities epiphany, my husband was out of town, and school was cancelled for the next two days due to inclement weather. My son was stuck with me, with no car and no cell phone. Day one, I asked him, "Walk in my shoes and tell me what you would do if you were the parent?" For that moment, he connected (or acted like he connected) to my parental responsibility to keep him safe, and he did homework and even applied to an extra-curricular activity for high school of his own volition. We had a good day. Day two, the kids woke up in happy moods, we had breakfast and lunch together, my son did homework and my youngest had a playmate over.

That Friday (when my husband got back into town), we took our first swing dance lesson. We noticed the YMCA offered a service two Friday's per month (for about four hours) of fun activities for our elementary schooler for a nominal fee so we could go out on dates. And that same week-end the weather was beautiful and we hiked, had brunch and window shopped in our eclectic downtown area. I was able to look at my kids and my husband and re-feel joy. One day at a time.

What gives and why, when you have so many relationship responsibilities? How long can some matters just be maintained until other priorities are tended to? How do you rank priorities? How do you sharpen your senses to notice helpful hints?

Adults being Self-Absorbed – Is that Enlightened Behavior?

If you judge people, you have no time to love them.
—Mother Teresa

One morning when I attended one of my meditative Yin Deep Stretch Yoga classes, I walked into what felt to be a bit of a chaotic environment. I was the first one there and the desk goddess directed me to another room for the class because there was a healer training workshop occupying the room we usually use. When I stepped into the next room she said, "Do you think this will be a problem?" There were healer tables (you might recognize them also as massage tables) on every wall, cluttering the room for the incoming yoga students. We agreed that we could move the tables into the hallway if it got too cramped, and got settled in. One of the healers even walked by as we were getting settled and said, "Oh, we are doing some healing work…" not volunteering to remove them. The instructor for this class was wise, relaxed and kind as a general rule. She glanced at the tables, raised her eyebrow ever so slightly and we moved gently into our practice.

As we began our meditative yoga practice there was loud laughter and chatter, and doors not so gently closed. All of this time, these advanced healers knew there was a meditative yoga class going on, but were caught up in their own world. Happy to be together, there was chatter in the halls, loud conversations and just when I was about to get up and "remind" the group that there was a meditation yoga class going on I thought, "Wait, I'm achieving enlightenment in the moment! There was a lesson here and I was going to get the most out of my practice that morning because of the noise." It reminded me that noise is all around us (even in metaphysical, conscious living circles) and it doesn't always match up with what we envision as enlightenment. It reminded me to focus more intensely on how to go within while what surrounded me was more self-absorbed. And at times I am that same self-absorbed person.

This is actually in line with the way teenagers carry on. Teenagers are kids in developing adult bodies. They are absorbed in all the changes in their bodies and minds. That takes up so much mind time that they can't see past themselves to consider how they impact others. Some grow past this and can see past themselves some of the time, some think or pretend they can, some never can, and there are times when some lose themselves in environments or situations for periods of time. All these grays—Is nothing cut and dried?

Looking at something a bit more life intense, I had a friend that went back to work in the mainstream world as a retail store manager. She said that there were two primary philosophies that upper management promoted: trust no-one (theft was very high among employees and customers); and knock some heads to get and keep people in line. Prior to this she was a full-time holistic practitioner and teacher, and of course, her philosophy was the complete opposite. So how do you process that and walk a path of enlightenment? When in protection, self-defense or self-righteous mode, at times folks aren't as gracious.

I've been offensive and behaved opposite to what I view as enlightened. I will do it again when I get caught up in myself. And when I realize what I've done I have to forgive myself for being less conscious and move on. That could include doing some EFT tapping to remove the emotional charge (see my book *Healing What's Real* for more information), taking a mindful walk, breath work, yoga, and endless other techniques.

As we and others exhibit behavior that feels less than enlightened and adult, how much effort do we put into backtracking and apologizing to others when we have gotten caught up in "me" and not considered the "all?" Are others grounded enough to accept apologies? How grounded are we to take on the criticism when others call us on our "loss of consciousness?" Some become embarrassed and maybe even angry or indignant about negative feedback and then project fault onto others. How do we take all of this as expansive learning and less about being the victim or victimizer?

So the Theory is All Experiences Encourage Growth – Really? When?

The ultimate authority must always rest with the individual's own reason and critical analysis. —Dalai Lama

I had a girlfriend in elementary school that I kept in touch with through the years. She began dating a nice, honest, hardworking, guy when she was about 14-years-old, and married him when she was 18. She was surrounded by loving sisters and parents, they had two children soon after they married, their children completed college, got married and moved back to live close to my friend (their mom). She had a supportive, tight knit family that she adored and they adored her back.

Both of our fathers were alcoholics, so one of the things that we have in common is we abstained from over-indulging in alcohol or drugs. But when my childhood friend was in her (still under developed brain) twenties, and her kids were older and branching out, she connected with someone who was a drinker and partier and changed her outlook. I found this out when I attended a party she organized and she was drinking hard liquor shots. It was like this type of partying was a right of passage that she missed (she dropped out of high school at a young age as well) and she was filling in a life experience equation. Luckily she recovered.

My daughter, while in high school, jumped feet first into party mode. This same daughter had major weight problems (food addiction) when she was in elementary and part of middle school. Once she lost the weight her claim was, "Mom, I'm just trying to catch up with the better looking skinny kids' experiences after being fat and ugly most of my life." She was a size 5 women's in approximately 4th grade (larger than what she wore at age 19), but thankfully (through it all) she was committed to academic excellence and had general respect for others (well, except for me).

So teen or wannabe teen socialization seems to also include the need for mind altering substances for many (these types of substances are even more of a hallucinogen for younger, undeveloped minds). When partaking at any age, some feel more like they fit in, feel happier, or it takes the pressure off and helps some feel like they don't care if they fit in. How can we change the need to alter perceived realities with substances before teens adopt these patterns as adults?

I have some mind over matter ideas (you can read my book *Healing What's Real* on some thoughts in addition to upcoming thoughts in this book), but perception becomes what's real. It eats away at individuals as early as childhood. People are stressing themselves out in their own minds and are literally killing themselves, but not before they pass this on to their children. There are ways to move past pain and into places of comfort, but we can grow if we remember the lessons.

When it comes to teens (and even adults), realize that you will never get the full truth when they are going through "growth spurts." So the big question is how much of the half and non-truths can we live with as loved ones, parents and/or confidants to get through these periods as safely as possible? How much can we trust things will be OK and how much intervention is needed? On the higher spiritual plane everything is considered growth, but sometimes it's tough to put your finger on exactly what that learning is and when you've learned it. One of the keys is keeping a clear head.

Crystal and Indigo Kids – Are We Creating an Enlightened and Non-Enlightened Hierarchy for Children Now?

With realization of one's own potential and self-confidence in one's ability, one can build a better world. —Dalai Lama

Remember the first time you heard that your child or other family member could be "special?" Not just special, but major league tapped into the Universe special? And then the term "crystal" children emerged which moves beyond the indigo. Like Baby Boomers then Generation "X" and

"Y," kids today get millions of more visuals and audios than we did at their ages. All of them have always been special and now their developing brains have to figure out how to manage the stimulus and still focus on the moment at hand.

My teenagers just laugh their heads off at me when my elementary school aged daughter gives me any type of indication that she is remembering a past life. When she makes a statement, maybe while I'm driving, and I begin to quiz her on what she is "remembering," they start to use "my language" and poke major fun at me.

So what is it with the technology age, indigo, crystal, and all the "special" kids? I've told my husband on numerous occasions; thank goodness I can keep it simple and trust my intuition. If my guides want to really drive home messages, they nab me at dreamtime. I'm open to any information the Universe and my higher self feel I'm ready for, but I'm thankful for the ability to turn intuitive information on and off (especially if it is startling). But for children, this can become confusing unless parents and guardians acknowledge what they are experiencing.

For instance, I was talking to one of my visually (seeing dead people kind of thing) psychic friends and she said that when she's in a room full of people, she sometimes doesn't know who's dead or alive. She can figure it out over time if she really focuses, but she could be at a party dancing with herself and not even know it! The reality is, for most, the human eye only sees about 10% of what's going on around us, but we are still bombarded with messages and information constantly from the internet, television, and other stimulus. Our divine sources are getting the information to us constantly!

But back to our children, thank goodness that schizophrenia and other mental disorders aren't always slapped on our kids, because they allow their minds to remain open to see, hear and feel more. They will hold onto their connection to Infinite Knowledge if we encourage it. Many are no longer treating visions like schools treated left-handers in the early 20th century (forcing them to use their right hands to write and use a right-handers desk). Because folks, it's not just about "seeing dead people," it's about having out of the box ideas/visions that create a more organic environment, create alternative fuels, practice holistic healing, acknowledge the power of mind over matter, and much much more.

Parents do need mainstream language to deal with metaphysical matters in our schools so our children can be normal and intuitive. For instance, my youngest had an argument with another second grader and she asked if they could go to the counselor to work out their issues. After I read the school counselors notes, I asked her "Why did you think there was a problem big enough to go to your counselor?" Her response was in a nutshell, "I felt her bad thoughts so I asked if we could have an adult help work it out." When I talked to the counselor she said she was very impressed with my daughter's reasoning skills and I responded (carefully) that my daughter takes on others' feelings as her own at times. Some parents have even bigger hurdles as their children clearly see other realms, but there is help out there to allow them live in the mainstream as well.

But now is the time that we must protect our children from school teachers and administrators who are unclear on how to deal with these bright, world-changing stars. Particularly those that decide drugging millions of our kids is easier than taking a more trained, individual, holistic approach to guiding children. Today's kids are more tapped into Universal knowledge, and we have to come to grips with the fact that they are smarter and more mature than we were at that age.

One of my Neuro-Linguistic Programming teachers went into a school to test the "academically gifted" kids and the "academically challenged" kids to demonstrate how to work with individual talent. He gave them both the same test. He gave the gifted class the test to review on their own then take, but with the challenged kids he made sure he communicated to their strengths taking into account audio, visual, or hands-on kinesthetic learners. When they took the test, there was no significant difference between the gifted and challenged class scores because he taught to the labeled "academically challenged" kids strengths. The lessons we are learning from these bright souls are countless.

Then these bright kids become teenagers. How do we help them tap into their talents? How do we help them all live a fulfilling, enlightened life?

Yep, I Can Be Bitter About the Parenting Experience

The moment there is suspicion about a person's motives, every-thing he does becomes tainted.   —Mohandas Gandhi

This teenager experience—Wow! What an eye opener. I'm really not my ideal self through some of these experiences. As I attempt to achieve an "enlightened" state as a professional and overall person, this experience has really challenged me on all levels. I was like a deer in the headlights when my first child entered high school. It only took weeks for her to transform into a monster and then my second entered high school two years behind her and my world was officially rocked.

Being a parent to teenagers, I can't remember being more angry and frustrated except when *I was a teenager* (in high school and college). And, being the empath that I am, if I'm not careful I can take on emotions of other parents with teenage drama.

A close friend of mine is a perfect example. Her teens had gotten so bad that they would leave on a Friday and come back on a Sunday (sometimes they wouldn't get home until the weekdays), skipped school, would sneak out of windows or sneak other teens in at night while my friend was sleeping, shoplifted, did a variety of drugs and alcohol, (of course) lied constantly, and stole money and property from her home. We talked, at least, weekly and I would find myself fuming with anger when I got off the phone. It was as much about jumping into my friend's energy to comfort and support her as it was being angry with her kids for being insensitive about what they were putting my friend through.

Here is where I have been really fortunate; my friend was a couple years and two additional teenagers ahead of me so she could give me a heads up. So my first pieces of advice are to find a support person or two (who are a couple teenage-parenting years ahead of you whom you trust and who have made plenty of mistakes from which you can learn).

You will find out a number of things when you have teenagers:

1. They don't give you any more information than asked for, and even then many times they will lie anyway. For instance, if your daughter asks, can I go with (one or two familiar and trustworthy names) to a sleep over? And you respond, who will be there? They will give names you approve of immediately. If you say, how many other people are there going to be and what are their names? You may get more information, or you may not.

2. If you ask your teenagers closed-ended questions, they will give you a yes or no. For instance, my daughter said, "I'm invited to a camp out at so and so's grandfather's farm, can I go?" I used point #1 and my daughter told me most of the truth then she shared that boys were also sleeping over. I became curious and tested my theory out and asked her accompanying friend, "Did your mother say you could go?" And she responded, "Yes." Then I probed deeper, "Did you tell her there are going to be boys there?"

And she answered, "No." I responded, "You are your mom's problem, but you (my daughter) are not sleeping over." She did get an extended curfew for telling me the truth (I'm sure not completely but close enough).

Now, when you continue to read through this book, you will find that many of my experiences have not been this easy to solve. Similar to some of my life impressions being from an abusive childhood, I have also hardened and become less trusting on certain levels when it comes to teenagers.

I've asked myself, can I be enlightened and less trusting of my teenagers and their friends at the same time? My answer, I am a spiritual being in a physical body. While I walk into the fire, this can result in less than perfect reactions and emotions, but (inevitably) my kids are safer.

What fires have you had to travel through while still achieving enlightenment?

Can You Give Too Much Information?

In this life we cannot do great things. We can only do small things with great love. —Mother Teresa

My teenagers cringe when their teachers send letters home asking for feedback on who my children are and how they learn. Hello… Mainstream Metaphysical Mom, Author, Mind Over Matter Professional and Holistic Healer here.

Here is an example of a letter I sent to one of my son's teachers when he began eighth grade (this put him at about 13-years-old) and his teacher asked "Tell me about your child."

Financially, Alex doesn't want a whole lot of things. The things that he does want are

very specific (a skateboard, a skateboard ramp, an IPOD, a computer game) and he has been trained to save his money to get items he is interested in. He generally has money (from allowance, chores or walking a neighbor's dog) because he doesn't have much to spend it on. He is very generous, however, and if not monitored would give his money to his friends, siblings, buy his family dinner on vacation. . . Alex will benefit greatly as an adult by locking in some of the money that he accumulates through smart, longer-term investments (instead of being 100% overly-generous or go with the flow).

Intellectually, Alex is very smart (yes, every parent thinks this of his/her child), clever, a free spirit in many ways. He is one of the few Liberals in the City of Powell and is passionate about specific political views. He has no tolerance for discrimination, enjoys a little political bantering when appropriate, and for 13 can be very esoteric/visionary. Alex can be very process-oriented, and even as a pre-schooler had a difficult time switching stations to the next program/event. The reason why is that he will follow a process maybe once or twice as designated but then re-create one that fits his style (but it may not fit within the confines of the classroom). He learns more easily through audio techniques, tactile is a close second, visual last (if combined with strong audio then he learns more quickly). He is a hands-on learner which means (to me) that he may be told that something works a specific way, but that will only be his "truth" when he experiences it fully in his own way (for instance, tell Alex not to touch a cactus because he will get stabbed and he will touch it to make it his truth). Alex said to us last year that he didn't understand why "A's" were so important. "B's" are just fine. While we have explained how colleges view grades, he simply can't take our word for this (the hands-on thing) and will have to experience this when entering a less competitive college (which may be a better place for him with his laid back approach). Alex is not "a jack of all trades," but a specialist in a few things. You'll find Alex has traveled many places in his current short life (to date). . . Italy, Ireland, England, Scotland, Eastern and Western Canada, British Columbia, up and down the east and west coasts of the US. This is a great hands-on way for Alex to develop into adulthood.

Physically, Alex has few interests outside of skateboarding. Alex plays violin and we would like to see him continue to play through his senior year in high school. His passion isn't very high for violin but he enjoys music and it's a good intellectual exercise to expand his awareness of diverse music.

Socially, you won't find many more social than Alex. Some may interpret Alex as being loud (especially with friends), but he isn't aware of his volume in-the-moment (and many times after the moment). While this is part of his charm among his friends, it can get him in trouble when it's time to be quiet. Alex can easily be a straight "A" student but he has slacked on his homework and gets "B's" in certain subjects. We believe that part of this is due to peer pressure and straight "A's" not being "cool," another part is his go with the flow/in-the-moment attitude, the other part is above-mentioned.

Spiritually, our family has a number of traditions that aren't shared with the more mainstream community. While Alex is straddling his teenage style socially, he is very proud of our family practices. He also understands that others may judge without seeking a clearer understanding of various paths outside of modern (20th century) Christianity in the US. Alex is aware of a great deal of his current life genealogy in connection with his American Indian background, as well as links taking his family all the way back to the Mayflower (William Brewster). We have a very close-knit family that observes many approaches to spiritual fulfillment. Alex can be very esoteric and visionary in his spiritual approach and is considering part of his college studies to be in comparative religions and multi-cultural architecture.

While there are many more facets to our son, this should give you a top-line view. If you have any specific questions, we'd be happy to answer them for you.

Am I a teenager's worse nightmare or what?

What my kids do know is that I have invested the time to understand them. That is, until they change again. I am an interested parent that helps teachers (if they want it) see my children in multi-dimensional ways. How would you respond to "Tell me about your son or daughter?"

Teen Talks in New Age Language –
Missed that Mark

Whatever words we utter should be chosen with care for people will hear them and be influenced by them for good or ill.

—Buddha

Sunday. What a special day. For me, usually the top of the list is sleeping as late as possible. Having a Cancer moon (this is also my North Node so a major influence as I move forward in my life), soaking up the moon energy then sleeping it off makes for an awesome day. To give you the setting of this particular day, my son asked for permission to go to the skate (boarding) park, my oldest had to be transported to and from her volunteer job as a candy striper at a local hospital, our youngest wanted to play (at a park with a friend), my husband had to do the grocery shopping, and I was ready to straighten the house, do the laundry and set up for the next season (transition from Halloween to the next phase of fall celebrations). The house emptied out by the time I was dressed for the day with exception of my oldest who I was going to drive to her volunteer job. It was a good day so far, but then…

My oldest girl's characteristics—a Scorpio sun sign, and she has 20 in the day of her birth (I explain this in my *Birth Mix Patterns* series of books)—are of an inward processor, intensely passionate, and can be perceived as cold and/or distant in approach to people (especially at 16 years of age). Our previous night teenage struggle was that her business was not my business. But in the same breath, she wanted to be taken to the mall to shop, go to the drug store for make-up, and demanded I schedule her driver's education classes right away. On this day, I found myself becoming less interested in pleasing my oldest daughter.

Happy to get her out of the house, as I drove my daughter to her volunteer job I came back to her comments made the previous night. I told her that her approach to loved ones (from my perspective) continued to seem distant and cold and this would impact her in other inner circle relationships as she got older. I explained that there was little left that I could teach her, but that she would just remember this conversation (a little Neuro-Linguistic Programming anchor) and apply it as she experienced relationships and comments from others she cared about. (Even as a baby, I gave her baby massages regularly as she didn't like to be touched or held from the day she was born. She cried constantly and inconsolably as an infant.) She reiterated that her business was not my business, and I rebutted that at that point in her life that was not true. Her position was "I don't need your guidance. You can teach your other daughter (5-years-old at the time) what you think she needs to know... I don't understand a word you're saying... This New Age language is beyond my understanding." My mainstream response, "Okay, then maybe you can understand this (as my Leo sun emerged), you're being a bitch. If you want my limited participation, just let me know about major things in your life like when you're graduating high school, graduating college, getting married, and having children, and I will leave you to your 'business'."

I was in a "be careful what you ask for" state of mind, but using that language could also have been my own "be careful what *I* ask for" (the joys of being out of control when dealing with teenagers). Only minutes after I dropped her off, my husband called and said, "Did you and Leslie just have an argument?" I responded, "Yes." He laughed and said she just sent him a text message on his cell phone to ask him if he would pick her up at 3:00 P.M. When he responded "Yes," she text messaged back "Thank God."

My husband and I began taking the position with our two teenagers that everything they are doing is to prepare themselves for their lives. We observed that selfless acts were few and far between at this age (at least, from our eyes). And when we thought about it, how did good grades benefit parents? Their good grades might get them scholarships, qualify them for better colleges, get them into the programs that they desire, and get them satisfactory, well-paying jobs. Does that benefit us as parents? Maybe for ego reasons it benefits the parents (living up to the family name, bragging rights, etc.). Sure, some parents (certainly, not the majority) pay their children's schooling 100%, so there could be short-term financial savings for parents. But as parents, we felt it was still up to us to influence our children enough to mold responsible, contributing world citizens.

So how do we truly benefit as parents? Among others things we learn about boundaries, the joy of giving and receiving love, and the learning we may not have been aware of prior to "Sunday experiences."

Interestingly enough, the night I wrote this section I was in our TV room and everyone had gone to bed. I was flipping through the movie channels and a little blurb came on with high school aged, young adults sitting around discussing how their parents should back off to allow them to grow independently. And I was re-living parental growing pains when one of the young men's comments was, "We're not saying we don't want our parents in our lives, we just need them to give us more room to grow independently." Wow, thanks for showing me this message (and on cable television nonetheless). The art is to define the word "independence." I'm still regularly confused.

Have you ever been in a situation where you thought you were communicating clearly to someone and when you were finished you were met with a blank expression? How did you remedy the situation? If you didn't, how could you have remedied the situation? Maybe you couldn't remedy the situation, so how did you move past that?

Are Liberals Capable of Establishing Rules with their Children?

An ounce of practice is worth more than tons of preaching.
— Mohandas Gandhi

As parents, who sets the most effective boundaries? I was at a get-together at a friend's house one weekend, and these are usually chat fests for me. What this group of adults had in common is we all had children around the same age. We met because our kids hung out, so this became a major part of our conversations. Ten years prior, our kids would have been playing on the living room floor so we could keep tabs as they watched an age-appropriate video, but we were now experiencing the joy of teenagers.

I saw a sign at my gynecologists office that said, "I'm not afraid of you, I have teenagers." And, at this gathering, we met a couple whose stories made my toenails curl. Their philosophy was "If teenagers lips are moving then they are lying." Their oldest was finally in her first year of college, and while school was only 30 minutes away from home, these parents invested another $10,000+ to allow their daughter to live on campus. Why? For their sanity.

I was at a parenting point where I wondered, when can I trust my teenagers? They lied so many times to my husband and me that I wasn't sure if I could ever let down my guard. So we bonded and traded stories like war wounds. Then, the bomb really dropped. They found out I was a "liberal" and the conservative Catholic (I'll say up-front that I am completely open to whatever gets people through their lives on a spiritual front) physician said, "How can you set any rules if you're 'a liberal'?"

Ouch. What could have been my most productive reaction to this? Mind you, their daughter was an absolute terror in comparison to ours (at least at face value) so should I have compared our tough situations to his tougher situations and said, "Well, who's got it mostly right?" No, I thought in my head. I shouldn't offend him (like he did me). I have to rise above this to show that I'm an open-minded, conscious thinker. So I said, "There's a difference in being a liberal, and being able to set healthy boundaries." In fact, "we" have a tendency to over process. You know, like when we decide to over chew our food to increase enzymes for digestion (I think thirty times is the magic number, isn't it?). OK, I couldn't help myself, so I shared an example of a boundary I set.

OK. Really, I wanted to politely shock the Catholics, so I shared this story. To encourage my daughter to really think about whether it was good timing on having sex, I asked her if she knew how to achieve orgasm without penetration (I've been told that many women don't ever achieve orgasm while having intercourse). I asked her if her boyfriend knew how to help her achieve orgasm, and did she know what her boyfriend likes (besides the obvious)? I also explained why she should expect to be satisfied.

Without considering her own pleasure, my daughter had this crazy idea that intercourse would make her and her boyfriend feel "closer." While it could be true (at least according to a magazine in my gynecologist's office) that when women have intercourse they release a hormone that is ten times more potent than in men and creates this concept of "closeness" for women, it's a real buzz kill when the guys are "finished." What do the guys do when it's over? ZZZZZZZZZZzzzzzzzzzzzzzz.

I even ended up asking her (virgin at the time) boyfriend if he knew how women were put together so that it could be a meaningful experience for both parties. He admitted that he really didn't, and I suggested that before he was to get "close" to anyone, maybe he should.

So how's that for a boundary? You think that I made my point? Are conservatives allowed to talk about orgasms, not to mention have them? (Well, I know the men are allowed to, right?)

I was very fortunate that my own first sexual experience was with someone (yep, when I was a teenager) that cared deeply for me, and I for him. I'd like my kids to have positive experiences, good memories, and experience pleasure and respect from their partners. What's a mainstream metaphysical mom to do?

Well, I spent and still spend a whole lot of time snooping into my kids' businesses and talking to them even when they really didn't like me to (which was most of the time during high school years). I can tell you that by the time my daughter was 18-years-old and heading to college, she talked to me a lot. I gave her my opinions, and she would regularly get frustrated with me and say, "Mom, I'm not going to tell you anything anymore..." (because I didn't always give her the answer she wanted to hear). But I told her—anchored with Neuro-Linguistic Programming—that she would always come to me because she knows that I will tell her what I think. I have her best interest at heart, I'm her mother and love her, and I'm not her 'yes' girl. She can take what I say, process it and make her moves from there, but I've taken her highest good into consideration to the best of my abilities.

How can you communicate to the subconscious mind of your children and grandchildren, or as you mentor children or other family members? Sometimes it makes the kids angry that I use the power of suggestion, but all's fair in love and war.

When Teen Friends Think You're Cool
– Flattering but…

Have compassion for all beings, rich and poor alike; each has their suffering. Some suffer too much, others too little. —Buddha

You'll see in other sections of this book where my teenagers say, "Mom, my friends don't approve…" or "My friends are afraid of you…" And my response is, "I'm not looking for their approval." But, the truth is I have enjoyed getting to know my kids' friends. Yep, they are liars, but they are funny, quirky, high energy, modern, interesting, while also being annoying, developing brained, "I think I can fool you" kids. As they become adult size (even though their brains have nearly a decade more of maturing), they begin to see adults as their peers. This is about the time when teens struggle with new boundaries with teachers, parents and other adults, and there can also be a similar struggle for adults.

Nearing 16 (driving age), and then 18, things change. And when I say "nearing" I mean when you hear teens say, "When I'm…" They've got their eyes on the target. As "When I'm" increased, my boundaries were changing every few months. I had been emotionally beaten up on numerous occasions and was figuring out what I couldn't stop and what I could. My question became could I keep the kids safe while still accepting that they have to make certain mistakes on their own to foster their growth?

My oldest was less than six months from 18, and she was headed to college the following year. She called to ask for an extended curfew. I told her I'd rather not, and she honored that and came home. I noticed immediately that she had a little buzz going, so I said, "How much did you have to drink? She responded sheepishly, "I didn't have anything to drink." I told her in a matter of fact way, "Yeah you have, you have a slight slur and I can smell it even with the peppermint gum you are attempting to mask it with." So it was (again) time to "have a talk."

First, I was glad that she didn't drive and her friend was the designated driver (completely sober), but I also told her there may come a time when everyone has had too much and asked what she might do then? And this was about the time that my metaphysical intuition clashed with my mainstream middle class ego saying, "What will the neighbors think?" I knew that she (like many teens) would continue down this path for a time, but felt she would come out of it okay. So I told her that I'd like her or any of her friends to call me to come pick them up, no questions asked if she or her friends found themselves in a pinch. I simply wanted them to be safe. She said, "Really? Mom I am so relieved. I feel like I can be a lot more open with you now. My friends think you are so cool (this is probably because I fed them and allowed them to come to our house pretty much anytime up to this point), and this makes me feel a lot better." She went on to ask me not to be mad, then told she'd had a couple beers the night before as well, but drank lots of water before she drove home three hours later.

So it was time to educate her on realities like you "can't water down beer after it has entered your digestive system." We went to the Universal Consciousness/the Internet and typed "blood alcohol chart" into keyword search. This website said that most states say that a blood alcohol level of .08 or higher is defined as "Intoxicated" (surf the net in your area). According to the chart, (it looked at weight, number of alcoholic beverages, and hours consumed) she needed to set a limit of two beers or drinks if she was driving (this was measured in one hour time frames and within three hours the alcohol would be negligible). This became our rule of thumb. Our new boundary resulted in me receiving a couple of calls (other than my daughter) to be picked up or asked if they could sleep over with no questions asked.

What was interesting is after our discussion, as I was feeling the love and the relief coming my way, my daughter said, "Please don't tell dad. I think he still sees me as his little girl." I told her that her father knew she wasn't sweet and innocent and was aware that she was experimenting. She still mentioned this to me on a couple of other occasions. She was concerned that her behavior would rock his world.

As a parent, I would love to say that my teen wasn't interested in drinking and other "grown up" activities, but there were 6 months to go before she was a legal adult (even if she wasn't allowed to legally drink). Keeping her safe had to take on a new meaning.

I have a girlfriend whose two oldest boys aren't partiers, and who haven't experimented with drugs, alcohol, or sex. She had been shocked when I've confided in her, not to mention thankful that she didn't have to deal with this type of reality. My sister, with five girls, just laughs and says, "Welcome to my world." There are no perfect answers, but this was my answer for the moment.

Have you had to make boundary transitions in your life with certain people? Did you allow your intuition to play a part in making new decisions? If not, would it have helped?

Helping Others Feel like Insiders

Loneliness and the feeling of being unwanted is the most terrible poverty.   — Mother Teresa

Reprogramming boundaries from child to teen to young adult has helped me with social practices outside of my family as well. There was a habit that I mastered when I "trained" my children on conversation etiquette. Maybe you've done this. When I was having a conversation with someone, particularly another adult, and my child would interrupt without asking to be pardoned, I ignored or shushed him or her. Later in their "tender" learning lives, we (my husband and I) decided to have some fun with our kids; when one of our kids started conversations with one of us, he or I would jump into the conversation and talk over him or her. When they'd get mad, we'd respond, "What?" This "eye for an eye" seemed to help them with the lesson, but there was another pattern that I became even more conscious of.

When adults are speaking amongst each other and another adult or two enter the circle, sometimes newcomers are ignored until the thought is complete. This could sometimes make an adult feel childish, not welcome, out of place, or unwelcome. In a perfect world, others wouldn't be wounded by this non-verbal action, but as it turns out this can be more offensive than interrupting, especially in Southern regions, spiritual gatherings, and among certain cultures.

For instance, two different friends of mine, who happen to be African American, brought this up to me (unprompted) on two totally separate occasions (and even 10 years apart).

In the mid-nineties, my friend said to me over lunch conversation that white people are so rude when it comes to welcoming people into conversations. He went onto explain that when black people are talking and, for example, another black guy comes up to the group, the group stops and greets the newcomer, catches him up on the conversation and then moves on from there. Ten years later, another neighbor shared a similar thought.

I notice in New Age groups that I'm connected with - that are either multi-cultural, travel, are big supporters of eclectic and world cultures, and/ or who connect to the concept that we are all one - that if a conversation is going on there is a tendency to make gestures that symbolize making room for a newcomer (at least in my circles). Maybe it's touching the person's shoulder while finishing a thought, a quick head nod, a reciprocal glance and nod, stopping to say hello then finishing the thought, giving a quick synopsis for the newcomer then moving forward.

My oldest girl played volleyball in high school, and she knew that I was cautious with extra-curricular team parent gatherings. Many of the parents were very competitive with each other, and that energy, with my empathic tendencies, could pull my energy down. There were, generally, a couple of Queen Bee's or wannabe's. So, if I did go to any gatherings I'd have to take on an open posture that wasn't threatening which (at the same time) also decreased my ability to block negativity. So this was a tough combination for me because I love to chat and take a leadership role in pulling people into conversations that may feel alienated. Unfortunately, that can be confused with encroaching on "Queen" territory.

So what I had to do, as soon as I got into my vehicle after any parent mingling, was do Emotional Freedom Technique™/EFT™, and began tapping to remove the emotional charges from those experiences, and then visualize myself "clean." So what is it? Are "majority" groups (which happen to be white in the US at the moment) just not embracing a gesture that minority groups use to welcome others into conversations to demonstrate kindness and support? Are we suffering from backlash of misguided parenting techniques? Are people blinded by their competitive or territorial natures? All of the above? Other? Regardless of why, it seems that when we are in less of a space of competition, we are more in a space of support. When our interests are to bring comfort to others, then it's no longer called etiquette. It's called being humane, loving, compassionate, kind, and welcoming.

Observe this for yourself. How do you want others to feel when you're in a conversation circle? How do you want to feel when you enter a circle? How do you want to feel when you exit a circle? How can you take a leadership in creating positive experiences?

Can Teenagers Have Consciences? When Do They Grow Them?

The human voice can never reach the distance that is covered by the still small voice of conscience. — Mohandas Gandhi

For an adult looking in from the outside, I might say, "No." But, with my two oldest teens I found two things: they both had to experience first-hand many things in order to decide if something was good or bad, and they both had incredible loyalties to protecting their friends.

For my first teen experience, it took about a year to figure out that my oldest was spending a lot of time lying and covering up for herself and her friends. To honor her request, I didn't put her many indiscretions in this book, but this came to a head when I told her that I felt I needed to hide any money in the house from her and her friends. She turned slightly pale and said, "I have never stolen from you" and broke into tears. The switch was flipped. Her heart was aching, and she didn't know what to do, or where to turn. She told so many lies that she wasn't being honest with anyone—particularly herself.

As her tears flowed, she explained that after I found out about "some" of the incidents from the previous summer, she felt like she wasn't a part of the family. Likely, part of this was because she wasn't coming clean and became more secretive (than usual for a Scorpio) which distanced her from the family. The other part was that my husband and I were caught off guard with these new experiences. What in the world do we do? This was our straight "A" student. How could this happen? Wasn't she smarter than that? We had to find new approaches with her, and this unfamiliar territory created distance for all of us.

While my daughter just wanted to forget a lot of what happened "last summer," and I allowed it for nearly a year, I finally said, "Come clean." She responded, "You promise just to listen and not judge?" I said, "Yes" knowing that all the cards had to be laid out on the table for the air to clear and the family to heal. Well, luckily no needles or sexually transmitted diseases were involved, but it was shocking. So parents and guardians, if you really want to know the truth, put on your seatbelts.

Many little problems surfaced like friends who wanted her (or that is what she claimed) to do things that parents wouldn't approve of, who she hung out with at school, and all the small things added up to big things. It took guts to draw boundaries, and even got to the point of changing peer groups. So I gave her a new excuse to give to her friends, "My mom is watching me like a hawk and I can't afford to get in any more trouble."

She liked that, and all of her friends knew me well enough to leave a slight chill in their spines.

The day after our "talk," as we were on an errand, just the two of us, she said, "Do you remember that time you didn't know where I was? Well, I was (somewhere we told her she wasn't allowed to be)." Little things were just being blurted out of the blue. There was nothing much to be done since the stories were shared a year later, but she got it off her chest. By the time we got to her senior year (phew), I told her to visualize the best year ever. And while I didn't get full stories, she shared enough of the pieces to keep the family connection intact. I took whatever I could get, and she gave as best as she could.

Eerily, my son went through very similar experiences his junior year. At first I was wondering if this was because we relocated to another state, but journaling my parenting experiences (i.e. writing this book) reminded me of the patterns of chaos just two years prior with his sister. Then I began watching other high school upperclassmen—drinking patterns, variety of drugs, sex, "phantom sleepovers" to cover up all night coed parties and other lying patterns, pregnancies, even kids dying—eerie became better known as "The Dreaded Junior Year." And to think that there was a day when I thought the kids turning ten was a nightmare.

Consider journaling about your relationship "ups" and "downs." Are you seeing any patterns one week, one month or one year later? How is that creating healing experiences for you and those you are connected to?

Kids Leaving the Nest –
All Talk without the Pocketbook

An idea that is developed and put into action is more important
than an idea that exists only as an idea. —Buddha

If you have teen turmoil then there will come a day when "I'm moving out" leaves their lips. My oldest was angry her junior year in high school because she was grounded so she took *the* stand. The first thing teens do is look for a slumber party situation—"I'm going to move in with Sarah. Her parents will be fine with it." So what's a parent to do, but to give your kids a dose of reality. First, "No, you will not burden Sarah's parents for two years because you don't like the idea of being grounded." Second, I put together a budget for her and a deadline on when she either stayed or left. Here are the estimates I shared with her:

Expenses To Live On Own

	Per Month	Comment
High School Lunches	50	
Rent	500	Must live in school district, have roommate for lower rent, or live in lower standard housing
Food	200	
Gas for car	75	
Cable/Internet	110	Possible split cost with roommate(s)
Car Insurance	150	
Car Expense	75	Save for surprise expenses
Doctor/Dentist	0	No insurance
Gas and Electric	150	Split w/roommate(s) to cut expense
Cell Phone	40	
Clothes/Health/Beauty Aids...	75	

Fun $—school events, out to eat	50	
Unplanned extras	0	?
Total Monthly Budget	1475	May be able to cut expenses by having a roommate(s)

The terms also included that:

- She would no longer receive allowance
- She would pay for all expenses shown on the spreadsheet as an independent student
- She funded her expenses by working while in school. It would take about 40 hours per week to live on her own if she was being paid $10 per hour.
- She would purchase a computer before leaving home since our computers were for those who lived in our household
- College was paid by her if she moved out while in high school
- At 18-years-old and still in high school, students must have parent signatures on all forms so she would have to work out how to handle this with the administration

She decided to stay at home until she entered college and served out her "sentence" of not being permitted to sleep over at anyone's house for the balance of high school. Her patience paid off as we sent her off to college to get a taste of independence on our dime. But even if you don't have as much to offer, sometimes it's as simple as just providing the facts. Do you want a roof over your head? Do you want food to eat? Then you abide by these terms. I've seen situations where teens leave then they come back, they leave again then they come back. I understand why parents do this, but it doesn't seem to give teens strong enough messages. Letting go and holding our ground is the toughest thing we have to do as parents and guardians.

Sharing Your Space — Proceed with Caution

Love and compassion are necessities, not luxuries. Without them humanity cannot survive. —Dalai Lama

So what happens when the tables turn and a teenager asks to stay with you? Or anyone asks to live in your home for that matter? With the many economic complexities, this is becoming more common.

At one point, we were considering taking in a teenager that was finishing up high school in the area (who was 18). But what boundaries do you put in place? I drew up a personal agreement that my husband and two oldest high school aged kids reviewed as well. While the young man ended up not staying with us, many have been interested in using this agreement as a template for their own situations. Here was the agreement.

FRED & THE PAYTON'S PERSONAL AGREEMENT

1. Fred holds a job that can pay the following expenses throughout the time living with the Payton's.

2. Fred must attend high school full-time, and go to school everyday (exception if really ill). Fred would be responsible for calling into school to record absence.

3. Fred must work out with the high school how to handle all paperwork, medical forms, signatures, any guardian signatures required throughout the year. The Payton's will not be signing any documentation for high school for Fred. Fred must work out logistics with high school administration on how to handle.

4. Number one point includes donating $50/week for groceries (which Payton's will shop for weekly with rest of family groceries) and Fred has full access to all food in the Payton household for all meals/

treats/snacks. When Payton's make meals, Fred is considered a family member and would be great to have Fred eat with us, but not required. There is a small fridge in the basement that he can use if he wants something unique only for himself.

Fred's Expenses To Live As Independent Student		
	Per month	
High School Lunch	50	
School Expenses	35	
Rent	0	
Food	200	
Gas	0	
Car Insurance	0	No car
Car Expense	0	No car
Doctor/Dentis	0	No insurance
Clothes/Health & Beauty Aids/Extras	75	
Fun $ - school events, out to eat	50	
Unplanned extras?	0	
Total Monthly Budget	**410**	

Work Requirement while in school: 20 hours per week at $7 gross per hr.

5. All food is consumed in the kitchen, or on the table top counter in the basement.

6. Fred keeps his room and the bathroom attached to his room clean and roomy at all times. This includes any messes that he may make in any other part of the household, including the basement area outside of his room.

7. Fred does the dishes and puts in dishwasher two times per week (regardless of whether joins for dinner). Note: Daughter does two days, Son does two days. Payton's may ask Fred to take out the garbage every now and again.

8. Fred will do his own laundry and is welcome to use all supplies in the Payton household to do this.

9. Curfew is midnight every night. All doors will be locked at the Payton household at that time. However, if Fred decides to stay out, Payton's are not going to police this. It would be nice to get a call to let us know Fred is safe.

10. Fred will not put our daughters or son in a position to have to lie to their parents (like waking them up to let Fred in the door because he's late, or other circumstances).

11. Fred finds his own transportation to and from school, sports and work. Please don't expect our daughter to do this as she is on a limited budget for gas and time as well. Arrangements can be discussed on certain situations, but this is the general rule. Bicycles are available to borrow for transportation for Fred.

12. Fred is welcome to hang out in any part of the Payton household, respecting the boundaries that each Payton family member puts on his/her bedroom.

13. Fred is welcome to use laptops to access the internet, but must share time with the other three Payton kids. Michelle's computer is off limits (in her office), but her laptop is available. We also have two printers for access to do school papers.

14. Fred can use the Payton's official home phone number for local calls. If long distance, please ask to borrow Michelle's cell phone. He can also receive mail or other deliveries at the Payton residence.

15. To balance Fred's moods, when off season for track/cross country, Fred must continue his exercise regiment to keep his spirits up and balanced.

16. Fred will stay with other friends when the Payton's are out of town.

17. If Fred has a girlfriend over, all doors remain open. No exceptions.

18. If Fred has friends over, he must seek approval from Karl and Michelle Payton. Midnight is when all visitors leave.

19. In connection with Fred, no sex, drinking alcohol, or smoking anything permitted in the Payton household.

20. No one in the Payton family expects Fred to entertain or be social. The Payton household is his household. It's important that Fred has his alone time and space.

21. It's important to the Payton's to have a relationship of mutual respect and trust. It's clear that Fred will also do his best to keep things positive so that this is a good experience for everyone. If something isn't written above, remember to use common sense on knowing what is right and wrong. If any of the above rules don't fit over time for Fred or the Payton's it should be discussed right away to keep communication lines open. If we are no longer in agreement, Fred should make other living arrangements within 2 weeks.

Signatures would include Michelle A. Payton, date, Karl D. Payton, date, FRED, date

Regardless of who you bring into your home, proceed with caution. Be clear on the roles you play in each others' lives. Follow your intuition. If anything feels uncomfortable, address issues upfront.

Addictive Behavior — Some May Be Blessings

All compromise is based on give and take, but there can be no give and take on fundamentals. Any compromise on mere fundamentals is a surrender. For it is all give and no take.

—Mohandas Gandhi

Middle and early high school, we had regular issues with our son being addicted to video games. Our biggest issue was that we couldn't get him off his butt to do dishes or clean his room, get to bed earlier than midnight on school nights, or do school work of good quality to get higher marks on his report card.

Here was the blessing. We knew where he was, he wasn't partaking in illegal activity, and he wasn't having sex. He played his computer games in the same room that my husband had his home office, and he had such a keen ear (an audio learner) he could even repeat his dad's technical work conversations to perfection. Another blessing was he was also aware of many conversations his older sister had about parties, drinking, and more.

Once our son turned 17 and his sister went off to college, he traded off addictions. Some nights he would dive into his video games for hours and we struggled with feeling secure because, while he was home, we felt he could be doing something more productive. Other nights he went out with his friends and we were glad that he was socializing, but he could come home looking and smelling suspicious. He enjoyed his part-time job—he made money, he got job experience, and he was out of the house but somewhere we knew he was safe. However, on numerous occasions, he spent all the money he made to the point of overdrafting his checking account. He had so many life skills to learn before striking out on his own.

Schoolwork was always a challenge. We enforced a rule, by his junior year in high school, that he kept a planner for homework and other commitments so we could review and keep track of him. If he didn't deliver (not coming home on time, not following his agenda book, average below a "B" in high school and college courses), his cell phone and/or car were taken for periods of time. Some say, treat them like adults, let them fail, that's how they learn. But how many broken pieces can they pick up while their brains are developing? These were daily tiring exercises for all of us, and I was counting down the months to his high school graduation so that he could be "the man" that he wanted to be. What reins should be loosened and which tightened? When? How? I was listening and watching for the signs. He was still reachable, still listening.

Have you ever (or observed someone else who) traded one addiction for another? How did that work out? How did you (or the one you observed) replace a pattern with something safer, healthier, and/or more productive? If the pattern was not replaced, why did that fail?

When You are Blatantly Lied to – Finding Your Happy Place

There are only two mistakes one can make along the road to truth; not going all the way, and not starting. — Buddha

It was the last day of school. My son (entering his sophomore year in the fall) walked in the door and announced that he was not going to work and going to play video games at a friend's house. He got nasty with me when I insisted that he go to work, and then the battle began.

My son is an Aquarian (out of the box, I'll do what I want) and Life Path 4 (process oriented, stubborn streak). PLUS he was a teenager— Lethal. So when I ran an errand for an hour and came back to find my son had gone to his friend's house anyway, I was not happy (to put it mildly). My oldest admitted that she was the one who drove him against my wishes because they felt like I was making empty threats and I would get over it. OK, "livid" would be the word that described where I was. So what did I do?

Well, first I texted him, and he didn't respond. Then with as much restraint as possible, I got into my oldest daughter's personal space and said (and I summarize), "Are you serious?" She gave me a lame story of feeling bad for her brother, that her brother badgered her, and that I would get over it, anyway. What? Wondering how much more willpower I could muster, I pushed her head with two fingers. She looked at me in shock and said "We don't hit in this family, we talk things out." I told her she was grounded as she was painting her toenails, and I swiftly threw all of her beauty aids in her bag, marched them up to her room, and told her to join them.

What's a mainstream metaphysical mom to do? We aren't supposed to push with two fingers. We aren't supposed to scream. But, "reasonable" was slipping away. How could they be so blatant? And how could they think any excuse was reasonable? News flash! I am the Mama!

This happened to be a pretty big day for me. I just released my book *Healing What's Real* in a big consumer campaign and orders were pouring in. I was so excited, and feeling successful in my business, but feeling (again) "less than" with my teens.

Thirty minutes after I sent her to her room, my oldest came into my office asking to explain her side of the story. *Really?* She and her brother completely disregarded me as a parent! She then went for a different approach (as if punishing me—such a Scorpio approach), saying that "grounding" meant she had to stay in the house so I needed to go get her books for her summer reading and her boyfriend was coming over since she couldn't go out. *What?* Is there a reason why our kids think they have negotiation power? *Seriously?* "Go away" couldn't have been clearer at that moment.

I called the friend's house where my son was "gaming" and told him that Alex is not supposed to be there, his sister drove him, and he is being irresponsible by calling off work. I got the boy's father on the phone and he said he would tell my son that he was being irresponsible in regards to work, should not have come over to their house without permission, and even drove him to our house on his way out for an errand.

When my son got home he came in to give me his "perspective" which included "he wanted to enjoy his last day of school and be with his friends." His claim was he thought I was kidding (note that his father/my husband also reminded him to remain at home). Is it that they just create stories in their heads so vividly that they really start to believe them? How could they lie so artfully otherwise? Answer, they just do.

My key to sanity was to kick him out of my home office (just like his sister) for the moment or he would also get the two finger push. To bring my energy back up, I went back to something that created more positive vibes—back to swimming in the successful introduction of my latest book.

My oldest took her punishment like a woman and served her sentence being grounded for the day (including no boyfriend). Then my son came into my office and ate a bowl of ice cream quietly (after dinner). Still on my business success high, I allowed him to stay and then he spoke (and I paraphrase), "Mom, I lied. I knew that you would be mad, but I didn't care. I'm sorry. Am I really grounded for the rest of the week?" So began the perceived teen negotiation. I asked him to think about if he were a parent and knowing his full intention, which included his son blatantly lying to him, what would be the right punishment? He said it would be a similar punishment, but he would be a much more understanding parent and probably not punish him as harshly (well, I opened myself up for that). For the rest of night I was getting back rubs, "Mommy, I love you," constantly following me around helping me pick up toys, wash dishes after I baked some bread, and lame attempts of him using hypnosis and NLP™ techniques saying, "I'm going to have fun at my friend's house tomorrow. Thanks mom for letting me go. Mom, your shirt looks really good on you. Mom, you look really young with your nose piercing, did I ever tell you that?" And other attempts without success.

Boundaries had to be set to nip this in the bud for future. He was grounded from his cell phone and texting. He was grounded from video games. He was grounded from going to see his friends. It was 5 days of torture for me, but follow-through was imperative. Easy—No. Took time—Yes. Patience was a virtue.

How do you respond when someone blatantly lies to you? How do you feel when they add more lies in attempts to cover their tracks? How do you pull yourself out of that negativity? Why is it important that you bring yourself into a more serene emotional space?

What if You're Not In Charge, but Should Step Up?

Truth is by nature self-evident. As soon as you remove the cobwebs of ignorance that surround it, it shines clear.
                                                    —Mohandas Gandhi

Have you ever wanted to give someone the benefit of the doubt? Or maybe you thought a person had a pattern of lying to other people, but he/she would never lie to you. We wanted so badly to trust, but when we let down our guard, we found teens drinking in our home (when we were actually in our room, asleep), and much more. I started using the term "make me proud" when they left the house to go out—NLP™ and hypnotherapy techniques to program in our teenagers' minds.

One of my friend's girls came to visit one summer. She had cool face piercings, sang and played guitar, and made new friends right away. She asked to go downtown to a smoking bar (called Hookah), and while my husband and I said "No," I felt like I should call my friend to double check with her. I'm not her mom, but it was my watch and my teenagers would not have been permitted to do this. The answer was still "No." Disappointment was high for this teen, but she got over it and made it to the next day.

Then she asked if she could go to a friend's house for a small get-together. Intuition alarm. She said it was a small get-together, and I wanted her to have fun so I said that I would drive her and talk to the mom to be sure all was well. But then I had a revelation, why was I doing this? I had three of my own kids to contend with, plus something just didn't feel right.

To keep tabs on her, I allowed her to borrow my cell phone when she left the house. At the end of one particular day I was running errands and needed it back. She had used my cell phone all day, and texted her new friends back and forth, so I read them. They went on to talk about the acid that was going to be at the party, inebriated minors, and told her to slip out of a side door when she got home for our curfew and they would pick her up. It was truly one of the coolest busts I had ever made for a teenager. I was practically giddy when I called my friend and asked for permission to call the other minor in question to say "This is Michelle Payton. I read your text messages, and 'x' is off limits." And I hung up.

My husband is much more patient and passive-aggressive and prior to my calling my friend he said, "Maybe we shouldn't say anything and see what develops." Nope. This was a big bust! I was swimming in my glory!

Later that night our teen guest asked if she could talk to me about the texts and made the statement "why would I ruin a good thing?" (meaning being able to visit us). My response was, "I don't know why you (teenagers) continuously shut doors of opportunity." She said she was trying to figure out a way to get out of the party without me being suspicious, she told them she wasn't going to drop acid, but half truths still point to lies, and this new friend was a bad influence. And bad influences point to car accidents, arrests, or worse, fatalities.

So, I couldn't be the cool friend. I told her that she wasn't allowed to hang out with this party girl without her mom being in town at the same time. She was disappointed and I was disappointed. It was a downer that made deep yoga stretches and breathing exercises a necessity that night.

Have you ever wanted to believe someone, but just couldn't ignore the obvious? Do you find yourself mourning, almost wishing you didn't know the truth? Ignorance is bliss, until it creates permanent damage.

Breaking up Emotional Storm Clouds – Activities that Encourage Others to Talk

If we want a love message to be heard, it has got to be sent out. To keep a lamp burning, we have to keep putting oil in it.

—Mother Teresa

Feelin' the love wasn't always consistent, but I took whatever I could get with my children. When my oldest became a senior in high school, certain realities began to hit. Going off to college meant she wasn't going to see us as much. And while I was the enemy at times, I was the only mom she had.

I mentioned earlier that she had some indiscretions. As a result I had, in her words, "ruined her life" by punishing her after I found out. But one year later the dust began to settle. She wasn't happy that she would continue to be grounded another full year from staying overnight at anyone's house for her senior year (because of the unlikelihood of her being where she said she would be), but she learned to live with it — a boundary her brother would also endure a couple of years later.

Her last year in high school she was motivated to return to play varsity volleyball for high school, her grades were tip top, she continued her volunteer work, her ACT and SAT scores were good, applications to universities were completed on time, and she got a job after volleyball season. The key to success was she didn't always have the energy to party (at least too much)!

And because she was home, she began talking to us more often— maybe out of boredom, maybe maturity, maybe the realization that she was leaving home soon. Her senior year patterns included coming into our bedroom and lying on our (my husband's and my) bed and talking to us about "stuff." During volleyball season she had lots to share (how she did, what she did best, what she needed to improve upon). She asked her dad and me for back rubs regularly during bedtime, and that was a great time to get her to open up. She even let her guard down and allowed me to give her kisses in front of her friends! That's huge!

Then our son started asking, "Mom (or Dad), you want to trade back rubs?" As we'd trade back rubs, sometimes he would participate in conversations if we asked questions just the right way.

Dinner time was reignited as an important activity when our kids moved into their teen years. There are numerous studies about families that eat together staying together, kids getting better grades… What it comes down to is that our kids are basically trapped at the table, and the only other thing they can do is chew or hit each other (and they did that too). I'll note that this worked as long as the television was off, but, as much as possible, we worked around the kids' schedules to get as many people around the table to connect as many times per week as possible. And, frankly, as much of a pain as they can be, they are a lot of fun to talk to as young adults/teenagers.

What activities have kept you close to people you love? What kinds of questions can you ask others so that they will share what's most important to them or what's on their minds?

Manifestation Training Ground – NLP, Visualization and Deadlines

Your work is to discover your world and then with all your heart give yourself to it. —Buddha

When the kids were "under teenager," we had a saying when they tried to split our decisions. If one of the kids came to my husband, for instance, and got an answer that wasn't the same as mine (or vice versa) then we'd say "I can't repeat after mommy (or daddy)." It was easy to catch when they were smaller as they would ask to go to the toy store, have some candy, things that we both monitored heavily as they were younger. But as the kids got older they got sneakier.

My son was laying around the house for a number of hours and I kept reminding him about his chores. When his dad got home, my boy quickly slipped out the door when I wasn't looking, jumped into his dad's car (with him) and off they went to drop him at a buddy's house. Or, better put, they were *about to leave* when I stopped my husband from pulling out of the driveway before my son did his chores. He was complaining when his dad came in and said, "Okay, just do your chores!"

But this became a much bigger issue for us as my kids were finding ways to create "Team Daddy" vs. "Team Mommy." My husband is a middle child and they pinpointed techniques to pull that middle child pleaser out of their dad. With the kids, he has a tendency to be extremely giving, playful and silly. Their objective was very simple: "Get my way." Their tactic: "Get dad to feel guilty that he is acting like my parent and not my friend."

We also found that they were using one of our negotiation techniques to steer us in their directions as well. When they were kids we'd say, "Do you want the peas or carrots?" Well, when they became teenagers it was, "Should I get this shirt or this pair of pants?" Even our youngest (by five years of age) was getting the hang of this asking, "When we're at the store should I get two toys or three?"

The NLP (Neuro-Linguistic Programming) anchoring techniques were plentiful in our household. "When I have my car (never if)"... and the old "I am so excited that I will be driving next volleyball season" visualization. Or "by November 27th I will have my driver's license" (clear physical manifestation with completion date).

Had we created manipulative, manifesting, puberty-stricken (and prepuberty for that matter), mind manipulating, monsters? Well, while difficult to swallow at times, they have learned how to manifest their realities by using their parents as guinea pigs. They set goals, they stuck to them, they established deadlines, or used language that had them visualizing new realities in-the-moment to manifest.

Can you close your eyes and see yourself clearly achieving a goal? If achieving the goal is not believable yet, how close can you get? Take that first step and reach for it. How does that feel?

A Little Lie Doesn't Hurt Anyone?

Morality is the basis of things and truth is the substance of all morality. —Mohandas Gandhi

My husband and I love to hear our kids ask, "Can I bring some friends over?" It's rare that they hear anything but "yes." Knowing our children's friends is one of our keys to success in keeping them safe. But that doesn't always guarantee it.

For instance, with cell phones we created a feeling that we had a life line to our kids. However these became tools in the web of lies at times. Just because they *say* they are somewhere, doesn't make it so. If we want to truly confirm where they are, they have to call from the landline so we can view the number on Caller ID. But that doesn't tell you what they are doing, just where they are at the moment. Talking to parents doesn't always work either. The really terrible teens have been known to disguise their voices to act like the mother or father. You might think I'm over the top, but I've experienced these all firsthand. So what we came to prefer is that they came to our house.

But, if they came to our house, then bags and jackets were checked at the door before going into the basement. At first we thought finished basements were "all that." We spent tens of thousands to update or add finished basements to our houses throughout the years. But be on the look out. Clear alcohol was smuggled into our house in water bottles one time and the big stylish handbags have carried large bottles of wine and other "beverages." Some parents don't even let their kids go into their basements anymore, and frankly many should just padlock them during impressionable teen years. Many kids just don't care that they are putting you (the adult) or others in harms way by drinking, smoking or having sex in your home, and others want to be seen as cool so snitching is out of the question.

Did you ever let your kids do camp outs in your backyard when they were little? Did your teenagers still think it was fun? Of course they do—but don't let them do it anymore as teenagers. They will call other teenagers (which includes the opposite gender), and sometimes they will sneak back into your house, without your knowledge, and once you are fast asleep, with unexpected guests. This makes it an even bigger teenage adventure when they "get away with it."

Case in point, when my rowdy twin nieces visited for the weekend (15-years-old at the time), they asked if we could put up the tents in the backyard. Visions of when they were little and cute popped into our heads and we said, "Of course." Big mistake! Once all adults (their mom, and my husband and I) were fast asleep, they called some "friends" who showed up with alcohol and, likely, drugs. Luckily, my oldest couldn't hold her liquor (she was only 16 at the time), and she vomited in no time. The nieces went upstairs to her brother (14 at the time) and said they needed help cleaning up the mess and putting her to bed. He said that, when he came downstairs, she was basically in a daze sitting next to her vomit. Her little brother shepherded her up to her room, told her to take a shower, got her to bed, and told her that she should just stop drinking because she can't hold her liquor. This was all happening while all the parents were lying fast asleep in our beds. We heard about this nearly a year after it happened and were in shock. How could we be so stupid! I am intuitive, why wouldn't I "pick something up?" Why wouldn't my "abilities" serve me now? It's called teenage parent denial. My teens would never do that. They are open and honest with us, right? Not!

Maybe your teens want to do the smartest things, but peer pressure is really potent. Some parents have a code lined up with their teens if they know they are crossing the line and don't want to participate. There is a delicate balance with this strategy because the parents can't "snitch" either. Their only objective can be to keep their kids safe. If a teen is talking to the parent on the phone (for instance) and other teens are listening, he or she can use a code phrase to mention over the phone like "Is your movie good?" or "Is dad feeling okay?" Then you can be the heavy and "demand" that you pick your son or daughter up, or (if they are driving) that he or she drives home right then and there. But you have to have teens that are willing to walk away from socializing or parties. I didn't drink or smoke as a teen, but I was open to going to parties to flirt with boys, and social places to hang out.

Do you remember wishing that you had a way out of a situation, but peer or other pressure kept you from leaving? Why did people push you to stay? Why did you stay? Or maybe you're the party organizer. To get your party started, who did you pressure to "have fun?" As a spiritual being, what does that mean to you today?

Being Transparent – the Truth, the Whole Truth and Nothing but the Truth?

We do not need to proselytize (convert to another opinion) either by our speech or by our writing. We can only do so really with our lives. Let our lives be open books for all to study.

—Mohandas Gandhi

If you have teenagers or teenager wannabe's (12 or under), make sure all doors remain open when they have "guests." It doesn't matter what gender. Even with doors open (like your finished basement), these "adults in training" will seize the opportunity to drink, have sex, and do drugs in your home.

I thought myself to be a pretty hip mom, that these kids would tell me the truth and respect my rules, because they like me. OK. That's your cue to laugh out loud.

Enter my creative and talented 16-year-old relative. She had problems in school, and I told her if she cleaned up her act she could come and stay with us for her spring break. At the time I lived in Columbus, Ohio and there is really nothing to see or do in Columbus except to see and "do" her new boyfriend in our area.

I reminded her of our rules, including the one of "doors stay open" when our kids have guests. Well, this—and other rules—did not sink in. Why would I even have had to say out loud, "No alcohol?"

It was nearing the last day of her visit, and when kids are in my basement I "surprise visit" every now and again. She had other friends over as well and, to my surprise, I looked down the stairs and saw the door to the extra bedroom shut. I barged down the stairs and yelled loudly, "I am coming down and opening the door and there better not be any naked bodies in there. If there are, I'm about to see them." I opened the door and the boyfriend laid on the bed claiming to have a Tourette's attack and he was dizzy and felt sick to his stomach, and my teen relative was in the bathroom sitting on the toilet with her head in her hands (she was on her moon cycle and claimed she had cramps). Intuitively I knew something was not right, but it knocked me off center when he came up with such a crazy story. How bad would I feel if I called his mother and she said it was true (interestingly enough I didn't know his mother so I couldn't call and confirm... a weapon in his favor). So I just said "doors remain open" and got him a Tylenol® for his "vertigo."

After all the kids went home, my guest fell asleep on the couch downstairs in the basement. My husband went down to straighten things up and moved her big shoulder bag and heard a bottle clanking. He opened her bag and there was a huge bottle of Schnapps that was half consumed.

Shocked, he decided to simply pour the rest of the alcohol down the drain and put it back in her bag. The next morning she said nothing and admitted nothing to her mother.

We talked to her mother, a week later, after we interviewed all the other kids (except for the boyfriend), and were told that "the boyfriend" was the only one drinking (Um, sure). But the plot thickened when we found out the Schnapps was found in our 17-year-old's closet! What?! Oh, the webs we weave. No one was telling the whole truth, but we were getting enough chunks to form our theory.

What is the mainstream metaphysical answer to this one? First, they are going to experiment. We did. They will give us some information, but not all because it's not cool to "rat out" friends. When intuition twinges in the slightest with teenagers, it's time to break up "gatherings." It doesn't matter if you are called "right" or "wrong." You keep your kids safe and send the rest home for their parents to deal with.

A note on "ratting" on middle school and older kids to their parents: Have you ever gone down this road? Be careful. Many parents don't like to face their demons (looking into our children's faces is like looking into a mirror). If you have any friendly connection/acquaintance with other parents that may end once "truth" is spoken, and you may be demonized immediately—partly because the parents are embarrassed and partly because the teenagers are playing their parents afterwards. Proceed with caution! Remember mainstream metaphysical followers, "we" process differently than the mainstream. In fact, we over process many times. Our New Age friends get that, but mainstream not so much. We are constantly reaching for "healing," and "enlightenment," and with that comes verbalizing. Using our "woo woo" language outside of our circles, many times, goes in one ear and out the other for "outsiders." No easy answers, but lots more questions.

To this day, my husband teases "This must be a Tourettes moment" when he hears teen lies. How can you create transparency in places that have hidden agendas in your family or beyond? How does your body feel when you hear something that doesn't quite make sense? If you can pinpoint how your body consistently reacts, how can you effectively move forward while not knowing the whole truth?

Messages Getting You Through Your Bad Day

All that we are is the result of what we have thought. If a man speaks or acts with an evil thought, pain follows him. If a man speaks or acts with a pure thought, happiness follows him, like a shadow that never leaves him.　　　　—Buddha

All said, I love that I am a mom. I love doing things for my family and most of our household money and time goes to filling their needs. There are days when it might not seem like I feel this way, but having a philosophy that all things happen for a reason says (to me) that everything in life truly has meaning.

March is a super busy month in our household as a general rule— Spring Equinox, Spring Break, two birthdays (husband and youngest) —but this particular year we were also planning for my oldest daughter's graduation and college entry, organizing my in-laws 50th anniversary, keeping the house clean for showings to potential buyers (our house in Ohio was up for sale), the anticipation of an offer to purchase our home, plus daily living, working and playing.

During this particular week my elementary school aged daughter was getting in all sorts of trouble due to talking and socializing too much in class, my high school son had an issue in school due to a teacher's lack of appreciation for his humor and (we'll call it) over confidence, and my college bound child had a new reason to believe that I was ruining her life. This time it was about possibly moving to North Carolina (7 hours away from the home where she grew up). It would "ruin" her summer because she wouldn't be able to say her proper good-byes before leaving for college.

Reflecting on my K-12 years, I was always noisy in school, and I was really self-centered. By the time I hit high school, a common phrase could be heard throughout the rooms of some of my more casual teachers— "Sizemore Shut-up!" I had a few boyfriends in high school that put up with a lot of my self-centered demands—poor guys. I really didn't know, nor did I care, about what was going on in my mother's or siblings' lives. And even with all of that, my sister and I today are the best of friends (the stories that she shared about her teenage years, you would have thought we'd lived in two totally separate households), my mom vacations with us all the time, and I have been happily married to my college sweetheart since 1987 (we started dating in 1982).

Being their mom, how could my kids not be interested in expressing themselves fully? They were born into a creative, out-of-the-box, independent, energetic family. Not to mention they have a more than comfortable lifestyle — regular family meals on the table, their own rooms, their own cars, and middle class personal amenities and schools. This has created more confident, socially capable kids, that cross many lines as they firm up their adult patterns.

As a parent, it's a new paradigm as well. How do I wean them into adulthood, still do my job as a mother, and effectively mentor them?

But let's go back to my particularly challenging day. A friend of mine dropped by in the thick of this chaos and I dumped my frustrations on her in 60 seconds or less. As I poured out my negative thoughts I felt weak and inappropriate. How could I be so blocked? What am I doing so wrong to create such an imbalance in my psyche? Then the messages revealed themselves.

I wore a Beatle's t-shirt that day that reminded her of a trip she made to the Rock & Roll Hall of Fame in Cleveland, Ohio. My learned friend said that there was a Beatle's exhibit that included some of John Lennon's K-12 report cards. Teachers reported (conceptually), "If John could just focus he would do so much better in school." Hmmm.

OK, breathe. Thank goodness for the small messages to gain access to the big picture.

Having a bad day? Are you wondering what "the reason is?" Those little messages will provide some answers. A song on the radio, a message on the television, a billboard as you drive, a phrase you overhear in a conversation, a line in a book. See it. Hear it. Feel it.

Big Memories with Simple Gatherings

We shall never know all the good that a simple smile can do.
—Mother Teresa

When I gave my mom a signed book (of *Healing What's Real*), I said, "Thanks for doing whatever you did to get me to this place." If you read my first book *Adventures of a Mainstream Metaphysical Mom: Finding Peace of Mind in a World of Diverse Ideas*, there might be a question as to why I said this. The answer is, good or bad I've made it to this moment and I like what and where I am. Whether my mom (or abusive dad for that matter) had a clever parenting day or not, somehow I made it here, talking to you, right now. And that's pretty cool.

I met my sister and mom for Mother's Day, with all our kids in tow, and my sister wrote in her card to me, "Can't wait until they realize how much we do for them and, out of guilt, they spoil us!" My sister is a real optimist, but I've said it before, stranger things have happened.

On this particular Mother's Day, we met on "the day" at a restaurant with my sister's five girls and one of the girl's boyfriends in tow, my three kids and husband, and our (my sister's and my) mom. We are an eclectic family and have a love fest every time we gather. When we get together the first item on the agenda is complimenting new facial piercings, ever-changing hair colors, clothes, make-up, and such. All of my sister's girls are 5 foot 10 or taller and are as loud as they are tall. My kids are even better at making noise (with just three), so it's like a kid/teenage chatty orchestra. You know, that constant roar of interruptions, giggling, whispering about their latest "I got away with" stories then loud laughter and comments of disbelief once the secret is out. My sister and I both decided to have one more child that was eight to ten years younger than the next in line. Between coloring, they mimic the older siblings, do some taunting and teasing, then make it back to kid games. Almost all girls, there are, at least, five conversations going on at one time when we gather.

The beauty of this is our teenagers (and even the younger two) really don't care that my mom, my sister or I are there (except when the bill comes), so we get to sit back and watch them play. Even as teenagers, they still want the ice cream Sunday bar that they got when they were little.

So while I'm not holding my breath that they'll really "get what we did (as mothers)," my sister, husband and I have built a support network for our kids so that they will always know that they have people who love them, and will support them. Warts and all.

What special moments are you creating to cement bonds in special relationships? Have you noticed the simpler you keep them, the more comfortable it is for everyone? If you have more complicated gatherings, how can you simplify them so that all enjoy them to their fullest?

Framing a Clear Reality with Personal Contracts

> *All wrong-doing arises because of mind. If mind is transformed can wrong-doing remain?*   —Buddha

My oldest teenagers, by about age 17 and 15, sometimes thought that they had decent parents. One of the biggest reasons my oldest daughter got to that space is because her friends were saying, "I love your mom... I wish my mom would be more like your mom..." This is when peer pressure worked in my favor.

Now, hear me when I say, these are the same kids that complained when I put boundaries in place as well. But they also knew, like any well oiled manipulating teen closing in on the legal age of 18, that this Leo sun sign mom responded extremely well to (people) sucking up. For instance, my daughter said to me once, "Mom, my friends don't agree with your parenting on..." And my response was, "I don't remember seeking counsel or approval from your friends" (the same kids that wished they had a mom just like hers). And I've continued to NLP frame over the years that my job is to keep her safe. I'm her mom first.

For our oldest daughter, our house had become a safehouse for a number of 16+-year-old developing adults. And one night, one of my daughter's friends called sobbing, "Can I stay at your house tonight?" I responded, "Of course, as long as your parents know you are coming here." She came over within 15 minutes and I sat and listened to her story. She had her perspective—and it was a valid one from her point of view then — I gave her some additional information to look at since she was open to it.

From ages 0 to approximately 13, the children we love, care for, and know are basically told what to do and how to do it—clean your room, do your homework, go to bed, get up and go to school, go run some errands with me, etc. As parents, mentors, caregivers, aunts, uncles, we are gliding along in our parenting patterns and then they hit high school.

At 13 or 14 the big changes hit, seemingly, overnight. Their peers are driving, having sex, doing drugs, drinking, working, going to parties that don't involve *American Girl* dolls or Legos®. Entering high school, both of my children became developing adults within weeks. We'd been able to successfully parent (let's assume) for 13 years, and in high school we only had a few short months to figure out how to modify our parenting skills for the next four plus agonizing years (and we suffered through reliving high school with them as well). Ugh!

While the young woman that came over that night was no teen-age angel (is there such a thing?), it was further complicated by her parents going through a divorce, having new love relationships, moving and selling their home, and reworking finances. They are already a bundle of raging hormones, so there's only so much any of them can take before their heads feel like they are going to explode.

After listening to the young woman's story, while she had no control over relationships coming or going, she had a very clear concern on being stressed about money. She was being required to purchase many of her essentials (women's hygiene products, shampoo, eye solution for contacts...), clothing, gas, and other items that she wasn't required to do before. While, for some of us, this would seem reasonable, this child moving to adulthood never had to do this until all the turmoil hit with the divorce. She had no idea how to tackle this, so it was reality reframing time.

As far as I could tell, she needed some type of communication device to gain clarity with her mother in particular. She needed a budget sheet to create a clear understanding with her parents, so I helped put together a budget showing the following:

Item	Who pays?	Per month Expense	Comments
Gas for car	Teen	$80.00	2 gas tank fill ups per month
Car Expense	Teen	$75.00	Save for major expenses, plus periodic oil changes
Health & Beauty Aids/Extras	Can parents pay?	$50.00	Contact Lens solution, tampons, shampoo, cleanser
College Application Fees, etc.	Can parents pay?	$62.50	Save from May-Aug. for fees need to be paid –Total 250 by Aug 2008
Recreation	Teen	$75.00	Movies, out to eat, school games…
Clothes	Can parents pay?	$75.00	
Savings Account	Teen	$70.00	
Total Monthly Budget		**$487.50**	
Money to make while school in session	Teen	$300.00	Approx. 15 hours per week working
Student can't pay for	Can parents pay?	$187.50	

The amounts and items are less important than the idea of creating a device for this young woman to open lines of communication with her newly divorced parents. What needed to be renegotiated to realign her life?

Divorced and "reblended" families are the rule rather than the exception. When lines of communication are a challenge, have you considered creating personal contracts to clarify intentions? These can come in the form of fun posters, handwritten notes on meaningful cards, even legal documents. Think about what fits your style, then frame a great reality.

When Children Die

It is a poverty to decide that a child must die so that you may live as you wish.   —Mother Teresa

But reality isn't always great. Over a span of just a few years, the school districts our kids attended had numerous instances where our kids had to face the idea that they weren't invincible—a teen died from "huffing," a first grader, a teacher, and three teenagers died in car accidents, and another teen was a suicide. The first grader and teacher were killed due to the careless driving of other people. For the teenagers that lost their lives in car crashes—two died due to the driver being inexperienced, drunk, high and then losing control of the vehicle, killing himself and one of the passengers, and separately one died due to texting while driving.

With the drunk driving incident, two girls and the boyfriend of one of the girls were at a highly publicized party with schoolmates. The boy was 17-years-old and past the legal limit of blood alcohol for a 21-year-old, drugs and drug paraphernalia were found in his car, and drugs and alcohol were also found in his system. I didn't know these kids, but it was reported that the passengers had no alcohol or drugs in their systems and they were of driving age. If either would have taken the wheel, I wouldn't even have a story to tell. The boy died, one girl died, the other survived with just a few scratches physically, but mentally devastated as she'd lost her twin sister.

Following the car crash, the school was in shock, but my oldest high schooler didn't feel this was the end of the trend. She shared with me that she felt bad about how she felt about the car crash and I asked her "How so?" She said, "I didn't think this was over." This came up because we were discussing another death (only four months later) of a junior boy who laid on the local train track and committed suicide. It's none of our business why, but what does matter is what others' learn from it.

Fall Equinox weekend 2008, my teenagers were excited about upcoming gifts (on Equinoxes and Solstices we give gifts to celebrate the coming season). My teens and I were going to the mall to shop for their Equinox presents and, when we had lunch prior to our spree, I asked them what they thought about the young man's suicide and how he died. I asked them what they thought about the candle light observance on Fall Equinox (harvest and rebirth season) at their high school and asked them if they were going. My oldest wasn't sure because she didn't know him. She felt because of the previous school year deaths, she should consider it. My nearly 16-year-old boy said, "I really didn't know him so I don't think it would be appropriate to go."

The day of the observance my son went and my daughter did not go. My son had no intention of attending until a few of his friends felt like he should come to support them as they process. When he returned I asked him how this impacted him. He said he was fine until his friend's mom said, "My father always told us, don't judge your whole life on one current event in your life." And she went on to tell the story of her dad losing his company and feeling like such a failure that he wanted to take his own life. But if he would have done that he would never have experienced the future successes, being paid thousands of dollars from businesses/professionals to speak and teach about his experiences around the country—to teach them about his failures to increase their odds of succeeding.

This brought my laid-back Aquarian boy to tears. When he got home he said, "Mom, can we trade back rubs?"

Here are some important facts to know. Suicide is said to be the eighth leading cause of death in the US of all ages, the third leading cause for ages 15–24, and fourth for ages 10–14 per the American Academy of Pediatrics and US Department of Justice. This collection of reports was released in 1995 and 1996 and at the time estimated that nearly 500,000 teens attempted suicide each year.

I was told by a counselor, who worked with communities of teens with a high suicide rate, that studies have shown that if you encourage teens to actually say the word "suicide" that this can decrease the possibility of a teen taking his or her life. The AAP and US Department of Justice have both recommended to speak the word "suicide" out loud when discussing the concept. I was faced with this issue and took this very seriously. Even if kids don't completely mean to follow-through, one careless move could lead to a point of no return.

I'm Liberal, but I'm Not All That Cool – Hipping Up to Get 10% Communication

First they ignore you, then they laugh at you, then they fight you, then you win.   —Mohandas Gandhi

Talking is what most kids don't want to do with their parents. And now it's all about technology. I mentioned earlier that we do our best to have dinner with our kids sitting at the table a few times a week. At first, it wasn't so much sports and student activities that got in the way as it was their work schedules. Then our oldest went off to college. Now what?

I insisted that my older kids get jobs by the time they were 14 or 15 -years-old to learn the value of a dollar and meet people that must work (many times more than one job). US child labor laws keep kids under 16 years of age from working past, basically, dinnertime. But once they hit 16 and have a car, most bets are off.

Dinners together become less frequent, but technology is here to stay and when I want to get in touch with my teens, cell phone text messaging is key. And when you are reading this book 10+ years from now, it will be another technology that kids have latched onto that you will have to learn to get in line for their attention. For instance, when our daughter went off to college, we added "Skype dinners." (Skype is a virtual phone call that includes video.)

I remember the first time I sent a text message to my daughter's cell phone. She was a high school junior and she thought it was so cool. She even showed her friends and said, "Look, my mom just texted me!" By the time my two older teens were in high school they had cellular phones, but when I'd call and leave voice messages they'd rarely listen to them. But if I texted they responded right away. If I have a long message, I have been known to text them and tell them to listen to their voice messages.

Some would say that technology is much too impersonal and meaning can be misinterpreted without verbal and non-verbal cues (with under 10% of communication being words, the rest being body language and voice tonality). But teens don't like talking on the phone either, so either way the meaning will be equally missed. 10% is better than 0. If that's all you've got, then go with it. They have half a dozen one-dimensional conversations going on at the same time and phones never leave their sides. During certain phases, you only get a few words out of them anyway. Keep up on their preferred technologies or lose out. Experiment and start communicating with their tools and see what happens. Don't communicate with their tools and see what happens.

Establishing a "Love Network"

We can do no great things, only small things with great love.
—Mother Teresa

If you keep a line of communication open (regardless of how), when more serious events transpire you (at least) have a cracked door to walk through.

The moving trucks left for North Carolina, we cleaned up our Ohio house and slept on the floor one last night— all five of us. In the morning we had to say our goodbyes to our 18-year-old. She was staying behind to work for another four weeks to save for college and to say her goodbyes to her high school friends (she stayed with a friend whose parents kept a close eye on their daughter so we felt as comfortable as we could in an uncomfortable situation). We drove in three separate vehicles (our son in one, my husband in one, and my youngest and me in the third) and I cried for about the first hour leaving our oldest behind. A couple of days prior I told her a story of how unbearable it was the first day I left her with a babysitter (when I went back to work). I cried all day at work. To increase my comfort I adopted a theme that the more people that love my kids the easier it will be for them in overall life. And this babysitter really loved my daughter. This is also why I arranged so many gatherings for our extended family. If my kids didn't feel like they could rely on me, they always had an emotional outlet with other loved ones. My philosophy—it takes a village.

After eight hours of driving, as soon as we pulled up to our new home (at about dusk) our 16-year-old son said he hated the house and the neighborhood (this was before he even got out of his car). Our vehicles full and our stomachs empty, we put limited essential items in our new home then walked to a local restaurant. Sitting down to our table our son blasted us—"I hate the area… the house, I want to go back to Ohio… I have a place to stay… What did I do to deserve this? …You aren't my mom and dad anymore," and on and on.

When planning and processing how this move would play out with my family, we discussed splitting the family for a while and even allowing my son to stay behind for two years to finish high school. Here was a blog I had written during this decision making period (at www. mainstreammetaphysicalmom.com)…

Receiving Anger Can Be Better than the Alternative

I am moving my family to Asheville, NC as I write this blog. My college-bound daughter is upset because she won't get to see her old friends as often. My second child is going to attend his junior and senior years of high school in a new state. And my husband is afraid we'll damage all of our kids for life, while struggling with his need for new beginnings and the necessary branching out to make new friends and develop new hobbies as we become empty nesters.

Many parents, partners, children, siblings, and friends leave familiar or loved ones behind as they "grow." Just take a look at the US divorce rate, and troubled youth statistics as evidence. It can sound terrible when I "write it out loud," but my momdar (mom radar) says better to uproot my family and deal head-on with the hurt, sadness, frustration, and even hatred that would be projected my way. Otherwise filters get clogged up with "My Wife or Mom doesn't want me/us" bitterness. Instead there is a transition that communicates "My Wife or Mom is walking her path and is taking me/us kicking and screaming but she wants me/us."

Many people walk away from situations without receiving others' truths (whether accurate or inaccurate) because they can't face UNagreeable processing. From the simple patterns of being unkind or superior to a waiter, a cashier, an associate, a peer (many times masking this with excuses for why others deserve cruel behavior), to leaving a love or blood relationship, too many "walk aways" leave a residue. It creates an accumulation of individual damaged filters, building groupings of calluses and downright nasty energy that affects the All Are One.

How much do you receive—not absorbing physically as your truth or even changing your action but simply hearing—to keep all processing flowing in a productive direction?

The move was my doing, my pushing, my dream (which included breathing new life into my businesses), and that came with a price. The first night that we were in our new home in North Carolina I quietly cried myself to sleep. While I knew it was the right move, many conflicts and struggles were to come. My son was distraught. We left our college-bound daughter to work for a month (being the first major separation of our family unit), and my husband was an emotional mess. I texted my daughter in Ohio and asked if her brother was communicating with her and she said, "Yes," and told him to give it a chance. My son was texting his friends (via cell phone) for hours that night processing his anger, sadness, loss, and hatred. And thank goodness he was texting extended family as much as teenage friends.

The next morning was a bit disconcerting and confusing as our son had a severe mood change. He came downstairs with a smile on his face. And as the week wore on he was decorating his room and his bathroom, he helped break down boxes, we went shopping, and he worked out at the gym that we joined within a few days of moving.

Then there was my husband's energy. It was way off... like a desperate energy that was primarily triggered when discussing the kids. I'd gotten used to his "we don't have enough money energy" and how to help him reframe that thinking. But this was almost needy with a bit of pessimist energy mixed in. And helpless wasn't the word that came to mind more than out-of-his-control discomfort. He couldn't fix things using past experiences and patterns. He had to clean slate his patterns to connect to his family.

Before our boxes were even delivered by the moving truck, my husband literally ran through the neighborhood looking for 8-year-old girls (looking for playmates for our youngest). He was stopping people in their driveways and on the streets asking "How old are your kids?" We started calling him "the stalker." I was beginning to get a little concerned that I couldn't drive my van out in the neighborhood for fear that I may be arrested for looking for little girls. But it was one of the ways my husband was creating comfort and getting back to some type of routine.

Change is inevitable. How does it make you feel when you can't immediately apply old experiences to new situations? What are some patterns that help you create comfort during transitions?

Bringing the Worst Out in Each Other

We can never obtain peace in the outer world until we make peace with ourselves.   —Dalai Lama

I didn't think I could have been sadder than when I left my oldest daughter in Columbus, Ohio when we moved (south with the rest of the family). That was until she came home four weeks later.

It seemed like we were moving into a more serene place after about a month. My 16-year-old son started his new high school and job, and was attending college as well (part-time). He liked his teachers, his courses, his job, and became more fun to be around. But when his sister and her best friend (also one of my son's good friends) came to visit for a couple weeks prior to their starting college, within hours a switch flipped and he became that horrid, cynical, disrespectful teenage boy that he was prior to our move (when I say prior, I mean he was like this for many years). Rebonding, our two older teens became a united force and ganged up on their 8-year-old sister.

When my son became his former cruel self, his little sister's feelings were extremely hurt over losing her kinder, attentive brother. Then when I asked him to do something that he would have gladly helped with since our move, he looked into my eyes with malice and used a tone that I had forgotten was a part of his behavior one short month ago. I had to leave the room immediately as I burst into tears receiving that former boy.

As I gathered myself, my older daughter walked into my office (being in our new home for less than 24 hours) and asked me to take her shopping, said she was bored, and needed to find a library to get some books. I simply couldn't collect myself enough to say (without sobbing) that she walked in being cruel to her little sister, and how she hasn't had the benefit of seeing what a great young man her brother was becoming because he took an "about face" when she walked in the door.

While my oldest daughter believed that her brother was just glad to see her, she was somehow bringing the worst out in him. His big sister had become an anchor for recreating that it was acceptable to be a bully to his sister and mother. I think the biggest disappointment with this reunion was that I expected, in reality fantasized, that having the family all together again would be blissful. I had this urge to load my oldest daughter into her car and send her back to Ohio so that I could get my new, capable-of-taking-on-new challenges, son back. So much more was to come over the next six months.

How did you create a new anchor in connection with people that didn't bring the best out in you? How did you create a new anchor if you didn't bring the best out in someone else?

Clearing the Way for Adulthood and Opening the First Door to Empty Nesting

The success of love is in the loving—it is not in the result of loving. Of course it is natural in love to want the best for the other person, but whether it turns out that way or not does not determines the value of what we have done.

—Mother Teresa

I am a bundle of contradictions. The difference between most of you and me is that I put them in writing for public viewing.

After my college girl was home for a few days, the dust settled a bit. When she came home, she brought her best friend, and for two weeks they lived the healthy lifestyle that we generally lead—walking, biking, hiking, healthy meals with a sprinkling of extraordinary sweets (my indulgence). We showed them a good time by taking them to the mountains, kayaking, downtown life, apple picking, and festivals, basically, every weekend for one reason or another.

Truth be known, I was campaigning for her to consider coming back to the area to work a summer job—and, after she graduated, maybe I could entice her to consider moving near the area. (First mission accomplished! She did come home for the summer.) What a contrast coaching my youngest daughter to get through third grade versus tempting my college aged daughter to visit as often as possible.

After they pulled out of the driveway (heading back to college), I finished washing the dinner dishes, cleaned the bathroom, emptied garbage cans full of make-up blotters, gum wrappers, old paperwork (What?! Why didn't she recycle those?!) and feminine products, cleaned mascara off the bathroom mirror (she gets this all over the mirror and I have no clue how), vacuumed and straightened her room for guests while she's not using it. I wondered, "Should I smudge again?"

Wait! When she came home I wasn't sure how long I could take her mean Scorpio streak, attitude, and lists of all the things she needed from us to prepare her for college life. Within days, however, I had my family of five back. She became funny as much as annoying. Good company with interesting conversations as well as a teenager going through growing pains. I walked into her room, now with her finishing touches, and it felt abandoned.

Even more "out of body" was when we visited for the weekend and left her at her college dorm. Watching her walk away from us to go to her new home was unreal, even feeling almost impossible. My struggle: "Come Back!" "No, Grow and be Independent." "No, Grow, Really Come Back and Grow Later." "OK, OK, Grow."

I teared up when writing this and... Oh, wait, I'll be back. Let me wipe my eyes and pretend it's allergies. "What do you need honey?" "Your video is in the basket, but you have to read ten more minutes before you can watch that. We have to take a shower and wash your hair in an hour. ...Yes, I can make you a snack."

Oh, wait. I just got an email from my son's calculus teacher. Oh, great. He didn't do well on his first test? How am I going to approach this and get teenage cooperation?

Calling All Guides!

Okay. Where was I? Oh, right. I was adjusting to the energy of one less family member.

Have you ever had someone in your circle and then they aren't? How do you fill that hole? Time heals many wounds. Being busy heals even more.

Becoming a Mainstream Metaphysical Parole Officer

No one saves us but ourselves. No one can and no one may.
We ourselves must walk the path.   —Buddha

Kids have uncanny capabilities of finding their ways through new situations. The plus is, since their brains are still developing, they aren't completely set in their ways. The minus is they have issues behaving (by parental standards) because all the connections are still developing. And what transpired next was a nightmare.

When too many minuses accumulate, I pull in my team of co-parents—extended family, school administrators and counselors (in another chapter I refer to them as "love teams"). This gives the primary caregivers—mom and dad—the ability to get a second wind when trusted others step in. It's like allowing parents to sit on the bench and put other players on the field. Keeping key "co-parents" in the loop becomes increasingly important, especially when in crisis. Most parents can't watch over teens alone. The first six months in a new town were challenging for my son—new peers, new job, new places to go that we (the parents) didn't know about, and not knowing parents.

By month three, he had major issues with smoking and carrying paraphernalia in his car (which included carrying things for friends that didn't have cars). We found them, had him destroy them in front of us and throw them in the trash. We weren't exactly sure how to dispose of larger glass items that he had purchased. Do you just put these in your recycle bin?

At first we thought the move was bringing out his bad behavior until we visited our old home town (Columbus) and dropped our son off at his buddy's house for the weekend. He was overemphasizing that the boy's parents were asleep and to be very quiet (we realized later). More on that in a minute, but once we got home he announced that he was going back to Ohio for his senior year and that it had all been arranged. He said it was unfair that we offered this up before we moved and now we wouldn't let him do this now. Hindsight—We shouldn't have offered this up. We did this to soothe his pain in connection with the move, but we made it worse in the long run. It was more of a selfish parent move to put off the inevitable.

Once I had a good night's rest I thought I'd call the parents who had arranged for my son's extradition to Ohio. When I called at the crack of 10:30 in the morning, a groggy mom (that I really didn't know) answered the phone and she immediately said, "We didn't get home until late last night/early this morning." And that, "The boys must have loved being by themselves like bachelor's over the weekend." WHAT?! She went on to say that she's sure that her son would love to have our boy live there because "He is lonely because we are never home." REALLY?! 16?! That door was quickly closed.

Moving on, by months four and five he was threatened with suspension from college (he took college courses part-time while in high school) for smoking on campus (he was underage plus it was a smoke free campus) and because he had to be warned to put his cigarette out (because, he said, "The guy pissed him off"). But it doesn't end there. He was given a 3-day suspension from high school unless he took a smoking cessation course at high school for a separate incident. He took the smoking cessation class by my insistence even though his claim was that he didn't smoke which was, maybe you guessed it, a lie.

By month five he spent all of his earnings of $700 (we monitored his spending online) in about a four- to six-week period. He was treating friends out to eat, and he was eating out two to four times per day. Gas was only about 10% of his spending. More life skills training was in order—basic checking account tracking—a set amount goes in, the same or less goes out.

By the half year mark, our son had many friends and even a love interest, but was receiving some poor grades due to study and attendance issues. This included him waiting until the last minute to turn in his final college paper resulting in a "D" in his first college course. The professor said he had an "A" in the class but the term paper landed him the lower grade. He got lucky when she gave him a break and allowed him to do a special project (taking an 8 week evening class and requiring another paper) to change his grade, but it could only be a "B" or lower.

We checked his car and his room regularly for any indication of unacceptable behavior and I had gotten in the habit of checking his cell phone texts, and tracking phone numbers online (texting and phone calls) among other things. Texts that I read when he put down his phone (when he wasn't looking) included: "My parents aren't home so we can party here tomorrow."

I had become Detective Mom as things continued to snowball. Our son didn't come home until 4:30 in the morning one weekend (not to mention many other nights being late). It was frightening not knowing where he was, but he made his excuses including that his phone battery was dead. New rule: Remain in the house until the phone is fully charged. This was also the day I copied all phone numbers off his cell phone and texted EVERYONE he talked to if he was more than 30 minutes late. His friends began telling him, "Dude, make your curfew. I'm tired of getting texts from your mom."

But the ultimate event, and the last straw, was when parents showed up at our door saying that our son vandalized their son's vehicle "looking for something." There were terrible verbal exchanges, and I was an emotional wreck for a couple of weeks. As it turned out, he swore he was somewhere else and there was evidence that pointed in that direction so we supported his position. Many did not believe this, because his "friends" of just a few months pointed the finger at him because he had a car (they admitted someone else was involved, but wouldn't name the other person that was involved who was likely the true driver). But, for me, it was guilt by association and we told our son that he needed to contribute to paying for the damages.

Lessons, Lessons and more Lessons. My old feelings of his older sister's dreaded junior year, a couple of years earlier, were reemerging, but on steroids. A sense of dread came over me—will I have to go through this with our third? If so, a locked down boarding school would become part of her mix. My enlightened self was not up to any more repeat performances.

Pondering, was it the move to Asheville? Did our school district in Ohio not monitor our kids as closely? Were we not watching him as closely with his upper middle class Ohio friends? Were we blinded by the transition from kindergarten to high school and our minds couldn't wrap around how a bunch of sweet little boys grew up to be smelly little turds? What was also missing in the mix was his big sister (off to college). Had we not realized how much we relied on her to watch over him as well? I busted him with paraphernalia in Ohio when I was packing for our move to Asheville—how long had he been smoking with friends and staying places where parents weren't present? The good news is he got away with less in the North Carolina high school (with outdoor security cameras in the parking lot and a full-time security officer). The bad news was school officials and our family began to wonder if our son would snap out of this bad behavior before he hit a point of no return. What would it take?

I questioned what this all meant to my growth as well. One of the reasons I came to Asheville was to seek more enlightenment. How could I maintain my spiritual self while dealing with a laundry list of real world teenage problems? After months of turmoil, I sat in front of my altar and called in all deities that I was aware of and any that I wasn't. I asked for protection, more kindness and compassion in challenging times and my life in general, and to surround me and my family with love and light.

Frankly, I've had an aversion to using the phrase "love and light" because, in my circles, I find that it is overused and that had been irritating to me—people believe they mean it but their actions are inconsistent. But I REALLY MEANT IT. I burned a combination of sage, rosemary, and lavender and went through my entire house repeating my mantra and also cleansed each person in my family. Following the burning, I sprayed every room and family member with a sacred water that I created. I EFT (Emotional Freedom Technique) Tapped for fear for myself, and I was surprised by an emotion that emerged of feeling threatened. I tapped for feeling betrayed, and feeling afraid for my son. I remote EFT Tapped for my son, each teenager and parent that came in contact with these many stressful events, and asked that all higher goods be served.

When you are in a really stressful situation, who do you pray to or meditate with? What tools can you use to clear your environment and your body? What support network do you have in place in the physical? Consider putting a spiritual process in place to empower and protect yourself and those you love.

Ancestor Studies – Grounding in Who We Are in This Lifetime

No culture can live if it attempts to be exclusive.

—Mohandas Gandhi

Stronger extended family connections can also create strength. You may travel in circles that focus on the importance of past life occurrences and/or ancestors. The concept of past lives or reincarnation is that you were physically other people in other times and places. The soul energy never dies but chooses to pass from physical body to physical body to evolve into the ultimate spiritual "being," "One," or "God."

There was a time when I was frustrated with not knowing who I was in my past lives. I wanted to know what other amazing people I used to be. But if I spent my time reliving all those other lives, how in the world would I live my current life to its fullest? Like any following, there is the overboard group. My observations have been that some in this overboard group are unhappy with the unfolding of their current lives and they attempt to soothe themselves by reclaiming old carnations. Whether true or not, some become experts on their former embodiments, but are not as confident discussing their lives in the moment. Physical responsibility can be difficult—paying bills, collecting a consistent paycheck, showing up regularly for work—because they are not grounded in this lifetime.

To be clear, I embrace reincarnation and I have found it interesting to have glimpses at my and others' past lives, but I'm that middle grounder. Like many forms of spiritual practice, it is difficult to prove, and every now and then even I question if I am making things up during my own visualizations. So, as a result, I consider every visualization has valuable messages to enhance my current lifetime (regardless of who's history it is).

So why is genealogy an idea to enhance spirituality? Finding out who you are physically related to in this lifetime helps you own or ground yourself (in this lifetime). From famous figures to farmers, you learn your physical roots. Your life is a bit fuller because you belong somewhere. You are larger. You are connected to a group of physical beings and your only effort was being born.

This is like a physical interpretation of "All Are One" as you will find that you are related to nearly everyone (or someone knows one of your relatives) if you break down every branch of your family tree. The result? It increases your sense of humanity.

On my husband's side of the family they have traced his roots all the way back to the Mayflower. I have sterling silver utensils that were dug up in the backyard of my children's great grandfather (by marriage) when hidden from the Nazi's in the 1930's. He was from Austria and managed to flee the concentration camps (being Jewish). Then pan to, interestingly enough, my mother's German roots. Her father was the first American-born family member. My grandmother (on my mother's side) was raised Mennonite for part of her childhood. And on and on.

One of my challenges was to prove my American Indian heritage on my father's side of the family. My father was out of the picture for decades (and until his death) due to his alcohol, drug, mental and physical abuse patterns and (what was diagnosed) borderline schizophrenic behavior (now called bi-polar in some circles). So our first challenge was to find out his real name. We found out that his mother died when he was a toddler and the reason he was given to his uncle was his biological father simply couldn't care for him while working the coal mines in the Hazard, Kentucky area.

I'm digressing again, aren't I? So there were endless directions to dig deeper into our Appalachian and American Indian family history. Our Kentucky families were huge—up to 16 children in one family in some cases. But one area of interest for which I was looking for physical proof was the rumored American Indian heritage. I hired a genealogist and also went to the Internet to find a large "Sizemore" (my maiden name) clan that claimed to be related to a George and Aggie Sizemore that were married on the Cherokee reservation in Cherokee, North Carolina. When I contacted some of the Sizemore clan on the Internet, a number of the Sizemore's had no idea that my grandfather Sizemore was even born and others didn't want to remember him. He was the youngest of 12 which may have lost him in the shuffle, but there was also a scandal that had him on the run (or be shot) because he had an affair with a married woman (he was also married). They ran away together and didn't want to be found.

Further research revealed Sizemore's having enrollment numbers on the Choctaw, Creek Dawes and Creek Final Roles. Another organized group of Sizemore's had the boys take blood tests to successfully prove the DNA connection to American Indians.

All three of my children have been required to do family tree projects at school. My side of the family is from humble beginnings, but the feeling of belonging, and being from somewhere, gives us all a sense of something bigger than we are. This moved us toward a sense of oneness on a larger scale. And with my children seeing that they are connected to American Indian, Appalachian, German, Mennonite, Jewish and more creates a stronger acceptance of multiple paths.

My children not only know their ancestry but also know firsthand their aunts, uncles, cousins, nieces, nephews, grandparents, and inner circle family friends to create a sense of security and solidarity. They know each others' hobbies, current events, what types of clothes they like, favorite foods, restaurants, and desserts, and understand their idiosyncrasies. They have hangout stories, holiday and vacation experiences, have fought, laughed and cried together. To scientifically prove my point, a study was published by Emory University and UNC Chapel Hill professors that show "Adolescents who report knowing more stories about their familial past show higher levels of emotional wellbeing, and also higher levels of identity achievement, even when controlling for general level of family functioning."

What are your beginnings? Start from today and work backwards. How can that build your strength?

Seeding Traditions – Creating Strong Connections

Love begins at home, and it is not how much we do... but how much love we put in that action. —Mother Teresa

What if your ancestor connections aren't quite as clear? Then you have a great opportunity to create strong connections now. Remember to be in the now with your family still in the physical. Expose yourself and your children regularly to cousins, uncles, aunts, and grandparents to build confidence in their love network. Our children know and love many of their relatives as a result of a committed effort of our families getting together regularly. In fact, I overhead one of the neighbor kids say years ago, as our kids bolted from his house across the street to meet and greet their cousins that just arrived from Cincinnati, "Oh great, it's the cousin love fest."

Not all relatives buy into this as they get caught up in their day-to-day stuff, but know their histories for your own benefit. I really didn't know any of my grandparents, cousins, aunts or uncles. So I built my own traditions from scratch. For instance, every year we have a large gathering which includes family pictures by a professional photographer. It's held at one location the weekend after Thanksgiving to not interfere with "other" family obligations.

We may go a bit overboard at times as many family vacations and holidays include relatives, and we realized this when our oldest daughter got very territorial one year. We were planning out when we might cram in all the December visits and I said, "Well, Christmas morning we can have…" I was stopped in mid-sentence when my oldest (then only 14) proclaimed, "That's our private family time. That is just for the five of us." I gave a quick glance to my husband with raised eyebrows and responded, "Okay."

In contrast, for Spring Equinox dinner my oldest asked, "Do you mind if I invite a friend?" At dinner (as we shared our gifts for the changing of the seasons), she explained to her Christian friend what this special occasion meant to our family. This was very cool for me as a parent to observe, firsthand, that our tradition (while very different from her friends) consciously made sense to her and she could easily and comfortably explain it to her friend.

We keep gatherings as simple as possible so that they are easy to participate in. Our strongest circle of relatives live anywhere from three to eight hours from us. So I set up a calendar of simple events. We meet at various locations to connect, at least, every few months. Many times it's just for the day and we all go back to our respective homes. While I usually call, text or email multiple family members monthly to simply connect, to really get to know extended family a phone call or email isn't enough.

If you don't have an extended family, allow others to adopt you. One of my mom's close friends never had children, but she always wanted them.

She wasn't even blessed with being an aunt so she became an adopted mother in our family. She handmade my prom dress, we had my high school graduation at her house, my sister was married in her home, she even married one of my mom's closest friends (this male friend was also my brother's housemate for a number of years while he attended college)! To spiritually adopt an additional mother, father, siblings, cousins... requires the adopter to step outside of him/herself a bit. Especially if you're the mom and a second mom has been adopted. But this is yet another way to extend love.

Can you put together at least one simple event that will help you get to know extended family better? Did you know talking to friends and family once per week or more actually makes you happier? Who should you call, have lunch or tea with this week?

Top 10 Teen Success Tips

All things appear and disappear because of the concurrence of causes and conditions. Nothing ever exists entirely alone; everything is in relation to everything else. —Buddha

More stories to come, but when friends ask, "What helped your kids through the Teen years?" These are my basic thoughts in consolidated form.

1. Understand their personalities.

I do this by looking at Birth Mix Patterns (Astrology, Numerology and Birth Order) and then monitor patterns from there. To know this as soon as they are born will help you get a tighter fix on what motivates your children.

2. Be a super involved parent.

Know their friends. Ask questions. Turn off the television during dinner and talk about classes, their jobs, and their volunteer work. If you're feeling uneasy, trust it and monitor cell phone activity online to see who they're talking to and when (I had to do this with my son, but not my oldest daughter). If needed, you can put blocks on cell phones and locators (so you know exactly where they are).

3. Be clear on rewards and punishments and be sure to follow through.

It's one thing to threaten, but it's another thing to follow through. Standing by your word takes time, effort and (sometimes) money. You won't be popular, but when you give rewards they will be that much sweeter to your kids because they have earned them.

4. Create productivity through working.

Get your teens jobs (or volunteer work, see point #5) as soon as possible. They learn the value of a dollar, learn what they like and don't like about certain jobs, and it keeps them occupied and productive.

In tandem, consider life skills training as well, like having checking and savings accounts that they freely access. Monitor spending and mentor them on the banking process (this can get very expensive if teens aren't taught how to manage bank accounts, we learned the hard way of course).

5. Create productivity through community service.

If you don't want your children to work then have them do volunteer work—with you, the whole family or independently. It gives them more ownership in the community, keeps them occupied and productive. If they complain, explain that they must be involved in the community and if they don't like what they are doing then you can evaluate new volunteer opportunities together.

6. Create productivity through school.

Get them involved in school sports or other activities. My oldest and youngest daughters were interested in school sports and activities, but our son was not. It was that much more important for our son to work and do community activities when not taking any ownership in school. He did, however, develop some strong bonds with certain teachers and his school counselor. Use them as tools as well and let them know how much you appreciate them.

Strike the balance of helping them reach their academic potential, and when they have a lapse in judgment give them a soft place to land without enabling, while still helping them understand the concept of accountability.

7. Understand that kids lie.

By the time they hit high school, their friends (peers) mean more to them than family. Know where they are, who they are with, and what they are doing. Many times, you won't know the whole truth because they don't "snitch" on each other, but ask questions, watch for inconsistencies, and monitor their words and body language.

Also, be aware of the embarrassment factor. Sometimes your kids don't want you to meet their friends because they act differently compared to your household. Our son was being a tough guy and was concerned that our lifestyle was too comfortable to share with friends. I was the opposite growing up and was embarrassed that I lived in low income housing.

8. Understand that kids will experiment with smoking, drinking, drugs, and/or sex. Educate them. Put strong boundaries in place on acceptable behavior. And by the time they are upper classman in high school, check their eyes (no, red and glassy eyes don't mean they are "just tired"), the aroma's on their clothes and their breath, in their rooms, and in the vehicles they are driving. DO NOT allow them to simply run up their rooms or bathroom to clean up when they get home before checking

in with you. Big hint that something is up! And don't even get me started on basements (I've written about this in another chapter).

9. Know when you have to back off.

When they get really close to 18-years-old, you will need to reestablish new boundaries. "I'm 18" WILL come up. You will need to lay out certain boundaries if they live at home, if they are still in high school, and/or if they are in college.

10. Remember each kid is different.

It's natural to apply old experiences to new behavior, but it doesn't always work. You will have to test the waters here and there. You do the best you can with the information you have at the moment.

There are times when things can really go bad and more stringent rules apply (no car, no cell phone, legal involvement, etc.). Then there are times when things are really easy. Some cruise through with no karma to work out, and have really disciplined kids. Just being curious, ask them what they hear around school about the "bad behavior kids." Ask who is considered "cool" and what they do that parents may not approve of. Keep your finger on the pulse of your (especially minor) children's lives.

One of my "free spirited" friends shared her thoughts and asked, "Do you, as a parent, have the right to define success for your children?" She felt that my children, when exhibiting behavior that I disapproved of, could possibly consider that successful and labeled this "judging." As a mainstream and metaphysical mother, my position, until they are 18 and financially independent, I am judge AND jury.

What I found interesting, while there were numerous power struggles, both my teens and many of their friends said to me as seniors in high school that they wished they had a couple of more years to be kids. Sure, they were excited about graduating high school, but they had a new appreciation for simpler times. How can we keep things simpler while doing life?

III Building a Community and Conscious Thinking

A small body of determined spirits fired by an unquenchable faith in their mission can alter the course of history.
—Mohandas Gandhi

I received an angry comment from one of my videos on my website titled "Are Today's Kids Gifted? How to Educate our Children." In a nutshell, this person was very bitter when it came to children and felt they are all misguided.

As a mother of three dependent children (at the moment of writing this book) while simultaneously seeking enlightenment—there are days when I wonder, "How loose are their connections?" For my own sanity, I revisit the physiological fact that their young brains aren't completely developed until they are 25-years-old—you can listen and download the transcript (free) to "Tips on Mainstream Metaphysical Parenting of Psychic Children" by scrolling down to this interview in the radio clips section of www.MichellePayton.com. But when my high school aged child skipped one-third of the required school days and didn't think about the consequences, I wondered what electrical impulses could possibly be going through his head.

Yes. I know kids' (reasoning) frontal-lobe areas are the last to make connections, but how much can parents and mentors bear? Yes. I also know that my children are a part of my learning and enlightenment, so how do I grow while moving through 25 years multiplied by three kids?

Some of my observances include that the sooner teens find purposes, find a way to contribute to community, and have passions that serve the higher good, the better off our collective world will be. Then there is the matter of how I connect more with personal and professional communities outside of my children as I become an empty nester.

Let's take a look at why community and "the village" approach is important.

Are Liberals the Only Group that Gets Abortions?

Freedom is never dear at any price. It is the breath of life. What would a man not pay for living? —Mohandas Gandhi

With all the problems in the world, this one always gets a rise out of people. There must be checks and balances and having conservative and liberal opinions creates an important multifaceted life approach. A major point of contention between liberals and conservatives is the concept of abortion. Are "the liberals" getting all the abortions?

When I was in college, I accompanied a friend to a clinic so that she could terminate her pregnancy. Looking around the room, there were a variety of cultures and ages in the waiting area. And to my surprise, while I waited for my friend to return from her procedure, I recognized a director of a company (maybe in his late 30's or early 40's) that I worked for (a known conservative) and his wife waiting as well. Our eyes met, and without words he asked me to say nothing. I nodded and averted my eyes until my friend returned.

On the other spectrum, my son came home from school (his sophomore year in the conservative school district, prior to our moving to another state) and said "A junior announced at the end of the (high school) year that she is pregnant by a sophomore boy in the same school and they don't 'believe' in abortion so they are having the baby." My response was "Do they believe in adoption?"

There seems to be a variety of reasons for pregnancies to voluntarily continue or end. With 2009 statistics (easy to "Google") stating that 40% of newborn babies were born to unwed mothers, it seems that women in general (teens and older) don't always connect with fear-based reasoning that sex can result in pregnancy. And this can be equally applied to men and women in powerful and visible positions to the most destitute.

Inaccurate messaging has developed in the US on the meaning of "Pro-Choice." Choice means that some women have babies, some seek adoption channels, and/or some don't have babies. Choice means that there are options for the many women who don't have health insurance, who are poor and can't feed another mouth, that can't afford to take off two months plus of work to heal following giving birth, who have jobs that require them to lift heavy objects and bend, who can't afford vitamins and food to nourish their bodies while a fetus grows into a baby. Choice means that women in nonsupportive relationships are not forced to wear a scarlet letter and be the "half" that is condemned while many "men" move on. A sign of the times, did you know that a rock star got paternity insurance so that WHEN he got women pregnant the insurance would pay the women to go away?

Here are some facts to help us understand the demographics of those who choose abortions. According to www.Forbes.com "Who Has Abortions" by Peter Brimelow published 18 October 1999:

"A survey of 10,000 women undertaken in 1995 by the Alan Guttmacher Institute shows that abortion occurs widely among all races and classes. In 1995 almost as many white women from households with annual incomes above $60,000 had about as many of that year's 1.4 million abortions as white women from households with incomes below $15,000."

"...There are significant differences in abortion's distribution. Fewer than half (46%) of the women involved are white, although whites make up three-quarters (74%) of the population. Black (women), at 12% of the population, account for 29% of the abortions. Hispanic (women), account for 11% of the population, and are also disproportionate users of abortion with 20% of the total.

Differences in religious background... fifty-four percent of American women identify themselves as Protestants, but they had only 37% of the abortions. (This researcher draws the conclusion that) Since most black (women) are Protestants, this suggests that the white Protestant abortion rate is quite low. Roman Catholics are more likely to abort than Protestants: They account for 31% of the population and of the abortions. The small group of women who sternly professed no religion, 6% of the population, were responsible for 24% of the abortion total. Research: Edwin S. Rubenstein, research director, Hudson Institute, Indianapolis. edwinr@hudson.org"

Abortion Recovery International as of May 2009 quoted on their website that:

"Fifty-two percent of US women obtaining abortions are younger than 25: Women aged 20–24 obtain 33% of all abortions, and teenagers obtain 19%.

Black women are almost four times as likely as white women to have an abortion, and Hispanic women are 2.5 times as likely.

Forty-three percent of women obtaining abortions identify themselves as Protestant, and 27% as Catholic.

Two-thirds of all abortions are among never-married women.

Over 60% of abortions are among women who have had one or more children.

The abortion rate among women living below the federal poverty level ($9,570 for a single woman with no children) is more than four times that of women above 300% of the poverty level (44 vs. 10 abortions per 1,000 women).

On average, women give four reasons for choosing abortion. Three-fourths of women cite concern for or responsibility to other individuals; three-fourths say they cannot afford a child; three-fourths say that having a baby would interfere with work, school or the ability to care for dependents; and half say they do not want to be a single parent or are having problems with their husband or partner."

On contraceptives, Abortion Recovery International shares:

"Fifty-four percent of women having abortions used a contraceptive method during the month they became pregnant. Among those women, 76% of pill users and 49% of condom users reported using their method inconsistently, while 13% of pill users and 14% of condom users reported correct use.

Forty-six percent of women having abortions did not use a contraceptive method during the month they became pregnant. Of these women, 33% perceived themselves to be at low risk, 32% had concerns about contraceptive methods, 26% had unexpected sex and 1% were forced to have sex.

Eight percent of women having abortions have never used a method of birth control; nonuse is greatest among those who are young, poor, black, Hispanic or less educated.

About half of unintended pregnancies occur among the 11% of women at risk of unintended pregnancy who did not use contraceptives in the month they became pregnant. Most of these women had practiced contraception in the past."

In addition to demographics, by 2009 teenage pregnancies were on the rise while approximately $1.5 billion of government funds were spent on abstinence programs. That's another subject for another time, but there's lots of data, of lots of people, that make decisions for lots of reasons—Liberal and Conservative.

The Apocalypse or "US" Awakening?

He who experiences the unity of life sees his own Self in all beings, and all beings in his own Self, and looks on everything with an impartial eye.   —Buddha

Liberal or conservative, have you ever noticed the abbreviation "US" is "us?"—the melting pot of the world? The Democratic Defenders?

Many have developed theories about the "Apocalypse." The 2012 chatter and the Mayan and many other calendars ending on that specific year is just one of the many "gloom and doom" years that have come and gone. What does it really mean? Some talk "end of days," others talk major earth changes, and still others talk about awakenings of consciousness. I also have a theory. Oh, I know you're surprised. My theory is that our world is readjusting in "US (All Are One) Consciousness" constantly. As our pattern of believing in separateness—culture, gender, income, religion, nature, etc.—re-emerges on a mass scale, we get elbowed in the ribs to get our attention.

For instance, for some, it's when it hits the pocketbook. With America's financial downturn in the early 21st century and its impact on worldwide investors, this created "US" awareness. Living the concept of supply and demand on real world terms this became perception and emotional desire. If housing prices were outlandish in certain areas, it was because people *perceived* their values should be higher. Then the perception that supply is short and demand should be high was applied. So should we be shocked when people no longer perceived houses were worth twice as much as what they paid two years prior? Should we be surprised when the stock market drops within minutes of scandals, replacement of corporate leaders, and rumors—true or false? The last year G. W. Bush was in office, as he made announcements the news stations showed the stock market reaction (buying and selling) on-screen. Nothing fact based, complete perception. For some, this is the awakening.

Each time we get hit with an awakening incident and we don't "hear it" then another hits and another. Belief in any particular science aside, being kinder to the temple called Earth is just the right thing to do. And while the unpredictability of our planet increases (regardless of why), many seem to be following similar patterns of destroying the temple called the body through (most of the time, voluntary) obesity, diabetes, heart disease, high blood pressure, drug, smoking and alcohol issues that are more prevalent in the early 21st century than ever recorded. As these temples go farther into chaos, they will shut down. For some, these are the awakenings.

The modern day possibility of seeing and believing a prophet is walking on water has passed. Cynics would check for strings, and others would sweep this under the carpet to control global panic. But any kind of chaos shuts down the conscious mind and it goes digging in the subconscious asking, "What's next?" Enough things are hitting us square in the physical to put us into reflection and reevaluation mode to wake up our spiritual selves. We begin asking, "What's really important?" It matters not *how* we get there, only that we get there. And the awakenings will come in waves, and at different speeds.

So I ask you now, what's really important? I've gotten a bit closer to that answer during numerous experiences since the beginning of the 21st century. This included a Level One Hurricane that hit Central Ohio. Ohio! Nowhere near the ocean!

Perceiving Safe and Secure = Safe and Secure

Just as treasures are uncovered from the earth, so virtue appears from good deeds, and wisdom appears from a pure and peaceful mind. To walk safely through the maze of human life, one needs the light of wisdom and the guidance of virtue. —Buddha

We had a Level One hurricane (Ike) in Ohio—it was reported that this was the first time a storm like this hit in 100 years. This would make sense since the ocean is 600 or more miles away. Power was out for a week or more in certain areas of Ohio. USAToday.com reported more than one million were reported without power in Ohio, Indiana, Kentucky, and Pennsylvania.

My husband went out of town on business for the entire week. And my three kids were wondering, "How is mom going to react to this?" As I've "matured" my tolerance buttons are more developed than my loose cannon reactions (this is my continuous improvement area). Owning that everything happens for a reason, and my life is flowing as it should (which is therefore good), I have everything to be happy about. Maybe you've deduced that most of my intensity (in my 40's) stems from being the mother of two teenagers and my next-in-line wannabe. But I have another dirty little secret (well, I did until now)—it's an intolerance for counting on other people or organizations to solve my problems.

When the hurricane hit us in September 2008, we had numerous power outages that lasted for days at a time, which included loss of phone service. There were so many challenges that came with this—loss of food and communication on multiple levels, boredom and fear. My fear included that I couldn't care for my family—they would be hungry, in danger, too cold, too hot, and in harms way. And then there was the kids' boredom and my (apparent) responsibility to fix that.

So as my husband enjoyed all the conveniences on his business trip (yes, I know, it wasn't his fault, but he wasn't there to help so I was projecting), we were figuring out how to rearrange our daily rituals. But the net of this experience was that I took being self-sufficient and self-sustaining to an all new high level. I would ensure that we would have lighting at night, hot water, fire to cook, a working refrigerator/freezer, some type of communication device to the outside world (which turned out to be cellular phones)—and all else was relegated as "nice to haves." I felt like Scarlet in "Gone with the Wind"—"…We'll never be hungry again!" I was on a mission.

When our power came on the FIRST time, I went online and ordered:

- a solar powered/crank powered/battery backup/electric backup radio
- a solar powered/crank powered/battery backup/electric backup battery recharger
- a crank powered cell phone charger
- Coleman camping lights and backup bulbs (that ran on D batteries

and smaller lights that ran on AA batteries which are easier and
cheaper to come by)

- Flashlights that run on AA batteries
- 100-hour dripless, scentless paraffin candles to use if batteries ran out
- waterproof/windproof matches
- rechargeable batteries
- regular batteries
- a really good multifunctional cutting utensil
- tablets and liquid silver to clean water if water refineries lose power
  as well
- cases of backup drinking water
- 2 stand-alone heaters

Folks can go overboard (well, actually, my husband and kids did think
I went overboard), but this made me feel safer. I put these all in a water
resistant tub marked "Emergency Kit." We had a gas water heater so we
had hot water for showers and could use our outdoor grill for cooking.

When my husband came home a week later (when our power and
phones went out a SECOND time) I insisted that he purchase a gas
generator that would support our refrigerator, charge our cell phones, and
miscellaneous small appliances (even use our washing machine).

In the process I learned a lot about our electric usage. Did you know
that it takes more energy to support a 1250 watt hair dryer and curling or
flat iron than it does to run a refrigerator/freezer? Truly the "price" of
beauty. Anyhow, an important note here is that psychically I was feeling
anxious about putting together an emergency package for my family
and home office months prior to this incident. Every time I would say
something to my husband (prior to the hurricane), he would "yes honey"
me, and that was as far as it went. I should know by now to always listen

to my inner voice. I don't need to research why I feel a certain way, simply acknowledge, trust and act on it.

During this crisis (they would never admit this but), my teenagers followed my lead closely. I teamed up with my neighbors, we shared certain supplies (ice and batteries were the biggest challenges), and we took control of the situation. At least that was my perception and my perception was my reality.

Was there a time in your life that you perceived was out of control? What can you do to increase your feeling of safety and security? Starting small is fine, but start.

When Obama was Elected President — Who in His/Her Right Mind Would Want that Job?

The difference between what we do and what we are capable of doing would suffice to solve most of the world's problem.
> —Mohandas Gahndi

First, I'll say that once people declare a certain philosophy they are rarely swayed from that spot. The McCain and Obama fight for the 2009 Presidency was an emotional one. And if you live in an area that is fundamentally against what you (personally) stand for, it can be uncomfortable. (We seek comfort by finding like minds that agree with our definitions of "right.")

Living in Powell, Ohio (Columbus suburb) meant that approximately every seventh household was potentially liberal (Independent or Democrat). With Obama's platform being to increase taxes for those making over $250,000 per year in a failing economy, many of the professionals in my neighborhood were at risk of losing money when Obama took office. I understand people wanting to protect their livelihoods. It's natural, but we were entering even harder times.

To give you a sense of how ingrained this idea was in my former (Powell, Ohio) community, my second grader came home and said, "We (her second grade class) voted on who should win for US President and McCain won (Republican candidate)." And when she'd get mad at me and go on "mom attack," particularly during the last six months of the race for the White House, she said on numerous occasions, "Obama sucks and McCain will be our next President." She wasn't even 8! This became an almost evangelistic movement in my daughter's elementary school!

But it didn't stop there. As I walked out of the voting polls, one neighbor said to another, "The United States will go completely downhill if we have a black President." I was in complete shock. It's one thing to be conservative but entirely another to be a racist. How could this be? While this "gentleman" was retired, had he forgotten what century we were in? Clearly money did not make the man. Liberal or conservative, are people still openly judging others because of their gender, race, religion, or lifestyle preference?

When my son went to his high school (in our primarily Republican community) the day after the election his mood changed drastically from enthusiastic to frustrated. 15-year-old students were repeating campaign rhetoric fed to them by adults and advertising to express their disappointment in the election results—included but not limited to Obama was a "terrorist," he was "not a legal citizen," he "was a socialist," he "was a Marxist" (and later labeled "a Nazi")... My son sent me a text message via cell phone and said, "OMG, these people in this school are so narrow-minded." To keep from being sent to the office for disorderly conduct, he asked for a bathroom pass and sat there for about 15 minutes to cool off.

During this very sensitive election time, what we all knew was something new had to be done. While Obama may not have been your choice, the prior eight years with Bush (Republicans) ended poorly and, when elections rolled around, all party members distanced themselves from the 2000–2008 administration. Regardless of who got into office, it was a long road to recovery for America.

When Obama won the election, I truly felt like anything was possible. The electoral vote being more than double that of his Republican competitor (as well as winning the popular vote by millions), sent a clear message. The majority clearly supported change in a way that America ("US") and the world had never experienced. An entirely new energy had been set in motion, and I and my family were there to witness it.

After the initial thrill, the realization of just how big this job was going to be set in. Before Obama even officially took office, he was working closely with current and past administration to keep America out of a depression. January 2009 came and went and issues with the banking industry, car industry, stock market, housing market, healthcare industry, businesses closing or "right-sizing," job losses, bankruptcies, war, other international relations, and more snowballed. By his (one year in office) State of the Union, he announced that he wasn't expecting to run for a second term because what he had to do was going to be very hard (and definitely not politically correct).

The "jumping ship" trend continued as Obama supporters dropped like flies because the new administration hadn't solved the many problems overnight. But Obama clarified on January 27, 2010:

"Let me start the discussion of government spending by setting the record straight. At the beginning of the last decade, the year 2000, America had a budget surplus of over $200 billion. By the time I took office, we had a one year deficit of over $1 trillion and projected deficits of $8 trillion over the next decade. Most of this was the result of not paying for two wars, two tax cuts, and an expensive prescription drug program. On top of that, the effects of the recession put a $3 trillion hole in our budget. All this was before I walked in the door."

The big question was how could we fix our broken country—All of us? Most adult Americans had hard decisions to make, watched others struggle, and wondered "Can they (the government) fix it?" "Can businesses fix it?" "Can the everyday Jane fix it?" This was a time when we all had to put our heads together to understand how to help ourselves and each other. When the chips are down, what are the top three things that enter your mind? How do you put yourself in a more peaceful place so you can handle crisis with a clear head?

Forcing Your Life Choices on Those You Love – Is that Fair?

A "No" uttered from the deepest conviction is better than a "Yes" merely uttered to please, or worse, to avoid trouble.

—Mohandas Gandhi

So when do we, as parents, say "Time for me," regardless of what the kids think? Not just going for a vacation, or purchasing something for yourself instead of them?

Several years before our oldest graduated from high school, I began researching where we were going to move. Columbus, Ohio was okay, but I was ready for an area that had mild season changes so that I could do more gardening and walking. A place that was kind to the environment, and an overall healthy living focus. A place that had and tolerated a mix of cultures and lifestyles which also included a large metaphysical community (where I could also reboot my businesses). So I went to the universal consciousness, the Internet.

I hit the obvious spots first, Boulder (Colorado)—too much snow, Sedona (Arizona) and surrounding cities—too hot, California—too expensive. We nearly settled on Flagstaff, Arizona, but realized that while we have a West Coast "attitude," our family and children would likely remain settled in the East. We wanted to have easier access to them so I searched East of the Mississippi. Austin, Texas—still too far and too hot—but really fit the bill on most other fronts (very green conscious). Asheville, North Carolina became a choice. Mild seasons, gardening and walking nearly year-round, mountains but not overkill, sensitivity to the environment, protected forests, (while I'm in a heterosexual relationship I was happy to see an) open gay/lesbian community, numerous liberal arts universities in the area, a vegetarian association, weekly farmer's markets all over town, many organic type grocery stores and organic sections in mainstream grocery stores, many integrative practitioners and medical facilities, weekly drumming circles in the city, there are even recycle bins at their many festivals!

We visited the area many times, even rented cabins a number of times to have extended family get accustomed to the idea. And then we had to decide when to make the move.

When our oldest graduated, our youngest would be entering 3rd grade and our second in line was a junior in high school. Initially (before they became full-fledged teenagers) we thought we would remain in Columbus, Ohio until our second graduated high school. As teen incidents began to pile up (even to the point of my second in line not pulling himself away from his video games for my birthday dinner—this meant merely walking down our steps in our home and sitting at the kitchen table) I asked myself, "Why am I putting my life and profession on hold?"

Many family members were unhappy about our moving. We have been the epicenter of activity to pull family members together for Thanksgiving and other activities for decades. We were two to three hours away from most family when living in Columbus, Ohio. Moving to Asheville would put us five or more hours away from most extended family. My son, of course wanted to stay in Columbus to finish out his high school career. He didn't like the idea of change, but he could play video games anywhere, he paid little attention to school (hated it, in fact), and friends were always lower on his list if it interfered with his "raids" (this would take forever to explain, but basically he and his team of *World of Warcraft* virtual acquaintances would gang together to beat up a character in the game to gain points). But somehow he still maintained a "B" average!

About six months before our move, all of a sudden our son started socializing outside of school. He admitted that he thought if I saw him being active that I would put our move on hold. Then he hoped for the economy to remain in the crapper so no one would purchase our house. The year we put our house up for sale was the year Obama was sworn into office and we reached the all time lows in the US economy (or so we thought at the time).

But, it was time to make my New Age move. It was time to be all about me (the label employed by my teenagers if I did anything that wasn't about them). It was time to expand my consciousness and my work and drag my family with me kicking and screaming. And wow, were they!

New Agers have been known to move and assume everything will fall into place from there (it does, it just doesn't necessarily include three square meals a day at first). I read a book where a woman packed up her belongings and 10-year-old, left her marriage and all else (home, job, child's friends and toys, etc.) and lived in her car.

It was a bit more of a balance for me. Being mainstream metaphysical, owning a business, in a loving marriage since 1986, valuing my parental duties, and liking the idea of having a roof over my head, I planned for years. How do I get to Asheville?

After a number of trips to the area, I answered some key questions. How could my husband get approval to live in Asheville and still work for the same company? What were the schools like for my kids? (They're excellent by the way.) Where could we afford to live? What were the costs to move from Ohio to North Carolina? What would it take to make my husband as comfortable as possible with this move? (He really could stay in Columbus forever because it was easier.) Plan, plan, plan. And then I put my plans into writing and slapped it up on my Vision Board (this is one way I pushed my plans into Universal consciousness). It included:

- What type of home we would like to live in and by what date
- How easily my husband would transition his professional job from Ohio to North Carolina and by what date
- When our house would sell in Ohio and for how much

Then I had to see if the Universe and all its mainstream participants were going to play along. I laid the plans, had to let go and let whomever.

Have you ever wanted something that you knew would make others unhappy? What did you do? Why? What were the short-term ramifications? What were the long-term ramifications?

Prepping for Change – Is There Such a Thing or Are We Just Bracing Ourselves?

We think sometimes that poverty is only being hungry, naked and homeless. The poverty of being unwanted, unloved and uncared for is the greatest poverty. We must start in our own homes to remedy this kind of poverty. —Mother Teresa

My husband was shuttling my nearly 16-year-old boy and friends to yet another event, when our son said, "All my friends don't like mom, because she doesn't put family first."

I'll frame this for you—I was "not putting family first because my son would finish his last two years of high school in another state." Additional framing is "parents (or maybe it's "mom's") should set their plans, goals, dreams, needs aside to be of service (i.e. being martyrs)."

Most teens need their friends like they need air to breathe. So yes, it was going to be a big change. And none of us were sure when that change would come. For a time, my college-bound teen was on the fence. After all, she was leaving for college by the time we relocated. But what was my son accomplishing by remaining in Ohio? He was not thriving in this school district academically—his interim report the fall before we were slotted to be in another school district included a "D," and two "F,s." He was getting in trouble at school because of his sharp tongue and wit, had nearly gotten into two fist fights (that I knew of), and considered himself a tough guy.

If we were forced to move for a job, that would have shed a different light on the situation. My youngest child's friend had to move because her father lost his job. The mom decided that she wanted to make a quality of life move back to her home town in North Carolina, they purchased a smaller home, she got a job and had her husband look for a job once they moved. Instead of putting the "for sale" sign up in her yard, she kept this very quiet. When people would come to look at the house, she would just tell the kids (elementary school aged) that they had to run an errand. Once the house was sold, they told the kids they were leaving and were packed and gone within a few weeks. But moving because we wanted a better quality of life, which included mom stimulating her career while not being the breadwinner, wasn't a good enough excuse.

We agreed to tell the kids a couple of years in advance of our planned move. And frankly, it was torture. Should my husband and I have kept this under our hats until the last minute? Many discussions and comments of how my second teen didn't want to move projected onto my youngest as well so turmoil mounted.

Moving is tough for everyone for different reasons, but my son's biggest issue was being forced to do (pretty much) anything. For instance, my son is an Aquarian loner with some "stubborn" sprinkled in, social when he feels like it, out of the box (especially for the conservative area in which we were living in Ohio), yet a very process-oriented Life Path 4 which accelerated his stubborn streak. His social contact was as much about text messaging, Facebook, and headphones connected to various video games and IPOD, than in person. And when he started his second year in high school prior to our move, he called it "going to hell" for his first day back.

Emotionally and physically prepping everyone for the move didn't go well. And because everyone was in his or her mourning spaces, no one was capable of seeing how much I had to hold myself back from leaving without them (or maybe they did). It was everything I could do to keep my inner New Ager under control. I have had friends that simply uprooted and left everything and everyone. It was what "they had to do." But with years of preparing, my husband's good paying job was intact for our relocation, our house would be sold prior to our move, and my family would have a roof over their heads with a father AND mother.

There was nothing politically correct at that point. My son went from "I'll find someone to stay with to finish out high school" then transitioned into, "I want you to stay so I can finish high school here with my family." Then, "I'm losing my sister (his older sister was going away to college and she was his best friend), and now we also have to move from everyone and everything I know."

Okay, yes that was a heart-wrencher.

Bad, bad and more bad. What was I doing? Why was this so important to me? We were so safe in Powell, Ohio. Yes, the area was missing many things for me, but everyone else was happy. Why couldn't I (as my teenager termed it) "put family first?" What was wrong with me?

How have you handled knowing that big change was coming—new friends, neighbors, acquaintances, learn a new area? How did you experience it? How did your priorities shift? What would you say to someone that had to endure big change?

Clarifying Agreements – Sometimes "Your Word" Isn't Enough

Better than a thousand hollow words, is one word that brings peace. —Buddha

My son took on a punk character (dressed in black, hair in his eyes…)—part puberty, part anti-establishment and part natural transition to finding ways to separate from "mother." So when he was around his friends he took on this "I'm a cool tough guy" air. He had a huge payback with this behavior because his group of friends really fed into it. A couple of his friends couldn't stand the idea of losing him so they put a plan together to keep him in Ohio to finish out high school (which, of course, he was pleased that they cared enough to attempt to pull some strings with their parents).

After months of emotional back and forth's, I was tired. So, I talked to one of the friend's parents who also happened to be a dear friend of mine. She liked my son. My son liked her. He called her his second mom. She was open to having my son stay with them for his last two years of high school. When I asked my husband to consider this, I could see his heart breaking, but he hesitantly agreed.

We told our son that we agreed with his proposition and told the hosting family the same. As I gave him the news, I had to hold back the tears. But luckily he got the "bad ass" attitude, and I was able to redirect my emotions. It was time for him to decide. Should he stay or should he go? How much separation was he truly looking for? But once our son felt some sense of control, he said, "Mom, I'm toying with the idea. I haven't made the absolute decision."

The next step was an agreement between our son and both families. Here's how it read.

1. Alex holds a job that can pay designated expenses outlined on this agreement throughout the time living with the Smith's.

2. Alex must attend high school full-time, and go to school everyday (exception if really ill). Alex would be responsible for making sure Mr. or Mrs. Smith called into school to record absence so that he is not recorded as a truant.

3. Alex must work out with the high school how to handle all paperwork, medical forms, signatures, any guardian signatures required throughout the year. The Smith's will be given a temporary guardian document so they can sign documents that require a parent signature for high school or work for Alex. Items can also be faxed for signature to the Payton household in NC if advice is needed. (Note: We later found out that we would have to sign over our son to new guardians.)

4. Alex has full access to all food in the Smith household for all meals/treats/snacks. When the Smith's make meals, Alex is considered a family member. While it would be would be great to have Alex eat with the Smith's, this is not required.

ALEX'S EXPENSES TO LIVE IN OHIO WITH THE SMITHS

	Per Month	
School Food Service/Lunch	0	Payton's pay $50/month
School Expenses	0	Payton's pay upon receipt of document to pay
Rent	0	
Food	0	Payton's pay $200/month to Smiths
Gas	$50	Alex pays
Car Insurance	0	Payton's pay*
Doctor/Dentist	0	Payton's pay*
Car Expense	$50	Alex saves
Rumpke Garbage Collection	0	
Delaware Sanitary Dept.	0	
Gas of Ohio	0	
AEP Electric	0	
Cell Phone	0	Payton's pay
Clothes/Health & Beauty Aids/Haircuts/other	0	Payton's pay $50/month to Alex
Fun $ - football games, out to eat, movies, misc.	$50	Alex pays

Unplanned extras	0
Total Monthly Budget	**$150**

Work Requirement while in school: 27 hours per month at $7 gross or $5.60 net per hr. or 7-10 hours work per week

*Found out later that we would need to sign away our rights as parents and insurance couldn't be covered through our policies.

---

5. Note that there are no extra dollars for travel to and from NC for visits. If Alex wants to drive to NC to visit his family he should budget about $200 for gas and food to get to and from Asheville from Powell. Unfortunately, no money can be budgeted in the Payton household for continuous visits.

6. Alex keeps his room (in the basement) and the bathroom attached to his room clean and roomy at all times. This includes any messes that he may make in any other part of the household.

7. Alex does the dishes and puts in dishwasher two times per week (regardless of whether joins for dinner).

8. Alex will do his own laundry and will confirm with the Smiths how much money he should donate to cleaning supplies.

9. Curfew is 11:00 P.M. every night in the summer, and 9:00 P.M. on school nights (including for work). All doors will be locked at the Smith household at that time.

10. Alex will not put Smith children in a position to have to lie to their parents (like waking them up to let Alex in the door because he's late, or other circumstances).

11. Alex has his own transportation (with his car) to and from school, events and work, and he can be expected to run errands for the Smiths to help around the house (driving other kids in household to and from events for instance).

12. Alex is welcome to hang out in any part of the Smith household,

respecting the boundaries that each Smith family member puts on their bedrooms.

13. Alex is welcome to use computer to access the internet, but must share time with the Smith family and get permission, and can use for school papers. However, there are limits on video games in the Smith household that would need to be applied to Alex as well so guardianship is easiest for the Smiths. All electronics go off at 9:30 P.M. with bedtime at 10 P.M. during school. Smith's have "no screen" times on the weekends and "required" reading at night half an hour before bed.

14. Alex can use Smith's official home phone number for local calls. If long distance, Alex should use his cell phone. Smith's (Powell, OH) is his official residence where he can receive mail or other deliveries.

15. To balance Alex's moods, he must continue his exercise regiment to keep his spirits up and balanced.

16. Alex may have to stay with other friends when the Smith's are out of town (if they are on vacation for instance).

17. If Alex has a girlfriend over, all doors remain open. No exceptions.

18. If Alex has friends over, he must seek approval from the Smith parents. 11 P.M. is when all visitors leave unless approved otherwise.

19. In connection with Alex, no sex, drinking alcohol, or smoking anything is permitted in the Smith household.

20. No one in the Smith family expects Alex to entertain or be social. The Smith household is his household. It's important that Alex has his alone time and space.

21. It's important to the Smith's to have a relationship of mutual respect and trust. It's clear that Alex will also do his best to keep things positive so that this is a good experience for everyone. If something isn't written above, remember to use common sense on knowing what is right and

wrong. If any of the above rules don't fit over time for Alex or the Smith's it should be discussed right away to keep communication lines open. If we are no longer in agreement, Alex will make other living arrangements within two weeks.

22. Alex realizes that Asheville, NC is 8+ hours away so holidays and birthdays will not be celebrated together with his biological family. The Payton's will do what they can, but with business and family commitments in our new area, plus travel and lodging expenses, it will be very difficult to make regular visits to Ohio or pay for Alex to visit NC.

I had signature spaces for my son, my husband and myself, and the proposed guardians.

Again and again I revisited… should we have just not said anything about the move so he didn't have to be reminded that he was going to experience what he hated most—change? Should we have never given him this option?

His high school counselor, my husband and other trusted advisors said "tell them (all our kids) ahead of time." Intuitively, I felt otherwise, but I was the minority and followed their leads (particularly my husband) because this had to be a team effort. Continuous suffering would go on for another year, and the mixed messages were very confusing.

For instance, our son frequently said that he didn't like people, but he kept talking about how he would miss people because (at least) it was a known. It's the unknown that creates the torment—where to shop, to work, to hang out, to eat.

There are obvious big decisions that change your life and then there are the subtle decisions that sneak up and hit you hard—like taking a right instead of a left, driving to a friend's house or staying home. Moving to another state was similar to my push to have our third child. We had two children two and a half years apart—one girl, one boy, both healthy. Even my husband's very independent grandmother in her 90's said, "Michelle, why ruin it?" (She was a Sagittarian, first born girl.) But I could feel that baby wanting to join us in the physical so "tick tock" went my clock. Yearning for her, was like I yearned to move to this new area.

Did I digress again? So I put the ball back in his court. If he wanted to stay in Ohio, then there was his opportunity. Once he read the agreement document, he said "I don't want to do this. But why should I spend any time putting myself out there (meaning hang out with his current friends as opposed to being a loner) if all we are going to do is leave in a year?" My answer (while first said by Saint Augustine) was, "Better to have loved and lost, than to never have loved at all."

The Smith family kept their invitation open until December of the school year prior to our move. I really wanted to keep the family together, but if he truly wanted to stay behind there was a safe option. To my relief his response was "Their house isn't like ours." When I asked for clarification, he said, "Our house is 'feng shuied,' and clutter free, and 'aroma-therapied,' and space cleared." I offered, "Well I can help clear the space and see if you like it then." But he gained some clarity—he liked our traditions, and our way of managing the energy in our home—at least for this round. My kids made (and still make) fun of me all the time for the mainstream metaphysical rituals I have in place. But when I smudged a room that they were in, they simply lifted their arms so I could clear their energy as well. Unfortunately, the conflict wasn't near over.

When you've had to make a really tough decision and there were other people involved, how did you keep a clear head? Did you verbalize? Did you write information down for clarity? All of the above or none of the above? How did the other people react? What worked and what didn't work?

Paying Attention to "the Signs" –
Being an Energy Hypochondriac

On life's journey faith is nourishment, virtuous deeds are a shelter, wisdom is the light by day and right mindfulness is the protection by night. If a man lives a pure life, nothing can destroy him. —Buddha

After years of metaphysical exposure and studies, I had become a bit of an energy hypochondriac. It was 2009 and I was more cautious than I ever had been when looking for a new home. I was a junky when it came to how energy shifted due to historical events, emotions and circumstances of past inhabitants, vibrations from building materials, the importance of an East facing home (to feng shui), the numerology significance of house numbers and street names, phone numbers, and compatibility to my and my family's birth mix (astrology, numerology and birth order). Not to mention the mainstream concerns of good school districts, safe walking, home values maintained, and pleasant neighbors.

At the time, it was investment opportunity meets financial demise energy. This particular year, many houses were in foreclosure. A "great deal" became for me, what kind of metaphysical work would I have to do to get this space back to flowing prosperity? On one particular street we looked at, there were, at least, six houses for sale and the lion's share of homeowner's had been forced to vacate (they were being shown empty).

Viewing the houses, some really obvious "No Ways" were two houses that had a wall of earth maybe 20 feet from the back door (like the homes were built directly in front of a hill). Talk about your chi stopper.

In one "Earth View" house (both in different neighborhoods), you had to go up a steep hill to get to the front door, it was empty (no furniture), walking in the front door the staircase was blocking the chi flow, and there were some odd (as best I can describe it) "secret passageways." What kind of blinders were they putting up, or dirty little secrets were they keeping? I had teenagers. I definitely didn't need that type of flow.

The other "Earth View" had a great front porch, and was empty except for when I opened a closet on the first floor where there was a wedding dress. We deduced one of the reasons for vacating the premises—the ending of a marriage. Next!

Looking at homes in the mountains, you also have issues with sudden drops. All the energy running downhill or you are at the bottom of that hill and you know what they say about that. S@#% rolls downhill.

While my realtor was pretty open-minded, it wasn't always easy for her to put her finger on why a house did or didn't work for us. But we eventually did buy a home from owners, happily married, that had four young children (one of the parents being a pediatrician)—infant to elementary school aged. Our new street address was one of the most solid and grounded of all addresses. It inspired inner strength, dependability, financial growth and responsibility. To stimulate a bit more creativity and open-mindedness, we loosened it up a bit, by adding brighter colors, eclectic artwork, and lighter (in weight) cherry wood furniture (as opposed to heavy oak).

See?! So many things to think about to enhance our lives, but in this home it was easiest to put "remedies" in place (if needed) to keep the chi that we preferred flowing through the home.

Changing our phone number was a nail biter as well. Really, I can get out of control. My new work number signified idealism and compassion, and was a great service or health oriented business number. Voila! Plus it was a very lucky number. I could go on and on (and did), but the point is (regardless of your tools) intentions were set in the subconscious mind and to whomever else was "listening."

What have you done to change an environment to support your higher good? Look around the spaces that you live and work. Do the symbols and colors match up with your past interests or future growth? Loosen up energy by moving a few things. Replace a couple of old messages with new messages. Make messages relevant to you.

Good and Evil – Sweet and Sour

As human beings, our greatness lies not so much in being able to remake the world—that is the myth of the atomic age—as in being able to remake ourselves. —Mohandas Gandhi

In dream state, I was in a damp, old, manufacturing warehouse. It was very quiet and I seemed to be the only person there. I walked up some old concrete stairs and saw two long pans of cakes (two feet wide by more than twenty feet long each). The outside pan contained white cake with white frosting and the inside pan contained chocolate cake with chocolate icing. The white cake had been nearly all munched away, with exception to some white cake at the top of the stairs less the frosting. The chocolate had not been touched, but was beginning to separate from the sides of the pan. Making a ninety degree turn I was facing down to another concrete stairwell with the cake to my left. I walked down the steps and on my return trip, I found a large knife and ran it up the side of the pan so as not to damage the cake, but get some of the chocolate icing off the side of the pan for a little taste treat. I left a still perfect chocolate cake and wondered how long the cake had been there.

Then I walked into a very large warehouse studio-like room with no walls and many people. While the ceiling was very high with drab floors and walls, the people were in full color including a group of Christmas carolers—a man in a tall hat, women in long colorful dresses with full skirts and bonnets. Many were in other period (dated) clothing that reminded me of old Europe. There were lots of "little people" walking as if on a mission. While all were in small groups that looked very different from one another, they all had one thing in common: their interest to spread joy. A man in "common" old European clothes said, "We've been waiting for you. It's your turn to take over and begin the manufacturing. Everything is in place." I had a sense that we were going to push things out into the world that would be instrumental in helping the group. Our intent was to spread ideas like compassion, joy, love, peace and the like.

Eyebrows raised yet? Scratching your head? Hey, it was dream state! And the message, believe or not, brought me some clarity. People want to feel "good" and want to make as few mistakes achieving good as possible Many (sometimes ravenously) partake in what they believe is "the light," but instant gratification is not the biggest growth area. Taking time to experience life treats or journeys (the dark and the light... knowing good you must know evil), respecting the many ways of reaching the target, is the ultimate spiritual experience.

How are you experiencing the dichotomy of right and wrong, sweet and sour, failure and success? And is there right and wrong, sweet and sour, failure and success? And if you do, how does that impact free will? Oh, and pay attention to those strange dreams. All the images may not make sense, but the little emergence of messages can really make an impact.

Free Will – A Bit of Buddhism, a Pinch of Christianity, a Dash of Paganism, a Sprinkle of the Kabala, and a Bunch of Intuitive Faith

This is my simple religion. There is no need for temples; no need for complicated philosophy. Our own brain, our own heart is our temple; the philosophy is kindness. —Dalai Lama

Purists of structured belief systems can become incensed when pieces of their philosophies are adopted while others are left behind, but in the world of "cultural creatives" (Google this if you've never heard this term), this is an emerging pattern. In defense of teachers or leaders in organized faiths, serving the emerging multi-dimensional spirituality can be confusing with beliefs running in percentages—I'm a lot of this, a little of that, and a smidge of the other. Middle of the road people are attracted to spiritual communities, but on their terms—they listen, learn, and then weed out.

What is interesting, as I've exposed myself and family to the many philosophies or religions, is:

- Most say the same thing with slight wordsmithing to claim points of difference like we see on packaged goods.
- There is an "all or nothing" circle, and a "this fits for me with a bit of adaptation" circle. The "adaptors" could attend many "brands" of faith and be content.
- Many stand in judgment of others' ideas which can also result in discrimination while the adaptors move more toward the idea that we are all one.
- Many have power struggles and resort to war to prove that they

should be the world religion or philosophy so adaptors more likely have a hand in creating world peace.

If we say, just for a moment, that these points have some "truth," then:

- There is a benefit to acknowledging that everyone can be right.
- While "all or nothing" followers say that certain rules must be followed, the "adaptors" can create a more relaxed and open-minded society.
- All are looking to achieve a type of balance with a core value of love, to be loved and be lovable. Judgment, discrimination, power struggles and war in the name of philosophies will not get anyone closer to that vision.

Looking at historical evidence, it seems like claiming a finite label can be so stringent, if put in the wrong hands, it can decrease free will. This can also shut down a valuable tool—intuition—when following rules without question. With multi-dimensional studies, middle of the ground folks may be more effective community leaders. Why? Because they are more flexible in a world where only one thing is guaranteed—change.

Whatever your mix, combining a bit of Buddhism, a pinch of Christianity, a dash of Paganism practices, a sprinkle of the Kabala and trusting our inner voices has the potential to create an inner peace. Inner voice could be translated as being angels, God, Goddess, All That Is, Guides, loved ones that have passed, or other types of intuition.

Package it any way you feel comfortable, but how can you do that with love and compassion for ALL? If you are in the "all or nothing" camp, read through all the sacred texts in your faith. Do you believe every word to be your truth (don't take someone else's "word" for it)? Do you resonate with all views on women, minority cultures, and relationships (for instance) of your faith? Can you be okay with being a percentage? If you feel most comfortable in "all or nothing," can you be at peace with "tweakers?" How is free will a part of your mix if you are an "all or nothing?"

Women supporting Women – When to Fish and When to Cut Bait

Sometimes one creates a dynamic impression by saying something, and sometimes one creates as significant an impression by remaining silent. —Dalai Lama

Then there seems to be another percentage worth noting. It seems to be an emotional conflict between certain types of women. I still feel awkward with certain mainstream parents. Here I am an author of numerous holistic books, owner of an international New Age art distribution company, mother of three (two are teenagers), I'm healthy and in love with my husband of 23+ years of marriage (plus five years of dating). Shouldn't I be really secure with myself?

My youngest was in first grade, and we were attending an after school event. I envied my husband connecting with a neighbor guy, chatting about sports or our lawn and feeling completely fulfilled. These guys just patted each other on the back and walked away thinking "nice guy."

On the other hand, before I moved to my smaller laid back town, I could feel a bit anxious if one female neighbor, then another, and another surrounded me (front, side and back) because they put off energetic "sizing ups." My intuitive shield is not locked and loaded enough at times when this emotional battle begins unexpectedly. Depending on my energy level, I can kick into my "rapport" pattern to connect with a couple of people and block the rest. After all, our kids play together, we have something in common. But I notice when I ask questions to lead into a conversation, they can over think what I'm asking. While classic NLP would say to take 100% responsibility for your communication (verbal and non-verbal), sometimes its as much about others' projections (their junk).

For instance, it's interesting (to me) to understand people. One of the women was a medical doctor so I asked why she chose her field. She told me quickly and curtly and then the energy flat lined. I turned to the next neighbor and asked the mom that went back to school to get her teaching degree (she already had a bachelor's, master's degree and credits toward Ph.D. in another field) how her classes were going and said, "You are so educated, you are a lifelong student." "I guess so" was the response. Hmm, well, that didn't go very well. No paddles could revive the energy of that conversation either. I looked over at my husband and he and a male neighbor were just laughing and talking about nothing. Was there food in my teeth (I quickly ran my tongue across them with my mouth closed)?

I've heard women who don't like other women say, "I don't get along with other women. I like having men friends better." And it's not because of any sexual attraction, just because they are tired of thinking too much. They don't want deep conversations. And some women say other women are just too mean, judgmental, and spend too much time sizing each other up.

One of my mainstream, but metaphysically tolerant, friends believes it's not necessarily about the subject, but it's about our make-up, our clothes, our hair, our nails, our teeth, and/or our weight. Her theory is that some women think you're competing for men's affections. Even if my defense is that I've got a handsome husband (in my eyes), who also happens to be my best friend, that wouldn't count. To some personalities, it's "let the games begin."

A male friend of mine that I've known since elementary school brought his family to visit. I was (by this time) in my early forties, feelin' pretty good about myself, neatly dressed and had on some jewelry, and his wife said to me, "I am past looking good for (my husband)." My careful response was, "I do it for myself, not my husband. I like looking good." This is my very Leo (sun sign) woman response, with outward expression being equally as important as inward and clearly standing in my power.

There is definitely a metaphysical speak and look, and maybe I'm too far gone and can no longer speak certain mainstream code. Should I just give up? In the metaphysical community (which is eclectic in belief systems), there seems to be solid support for other women regardless of physical and non-physical qualities (as we are all in different expression and spiritual phases). Maybe it's because so many of these women understand the concept of "standing in their power" (not to be confused with the label "bitchy").

It feels like some women are confused when they are shown support. Maybe it's because they are already on the defensive. If we celebrate their achievements and decisions (whether it's to be home full-time with their families or to be a professional), they think "what do you really mean?" Complimenting them when you see them—"Love your shirt. Congrats on completing that class. You look like you feel great."—They wonder (and verbalize) if they looked terrible the day before. And if (they perceive) you look better than they do, it could get sticky. There was a time in my professional life when I actually "uglied down" because of the sizing up of corporate wives. I cut my hair really short, wore pant suits, plain colored shirts that would rarely even show my collar bones, and shoes that covered toe cleavage.

I'm finding, now closing in on fifty, that a lot of this is a waste of time. And it bothers me that (sometimes) it bothers me. So what I do now, is tap this emotional connection out with the Emotional Freedom Technique™ (you can find out more about this in my book *Healing What's Real* or my YouTube EFT video). It can take about 5 minutes or more depending on what other emotions I'm working with.

You are who you are so how are you standing in your power? Who is your woman support group? How can you show support for other women? How can you push out the negativity that comes with some women's unjustifiable judgments?

IV. Achieving Health and Conscious Thinking

The biggest disease today is not leprosy or tuberculosis, but rather the feeling of being unwanted.   —Mother Teresa

Then there is the body. Some feel like the body has an "on and off" switch—you have this physical ailment, take this pill. I heard an interesting statistic in 2010 (Does anyone else love Doctor Oz?) that 90% of all doctor visits are connected to stress related diseases. What's stress? Emotional responses.

I have come to a point where I see the body as having an emotional response to "everything" we do. Yep, I said everything and that is a strong word. Emotions can be at the beginning, the middle, and/or ending. Emotions can be the lasting impression and trigger to stress and relaxation, sadness and happiness. Emotions can be anchors that make things better or worse. This depletes or nourishes your body, increases or lowers your immune system, which can then open or close doors to physical ailments and open doors to optimal health.

Can respecting your body be considered enlightenment? And if it is, should we put processes in place to encourage others to experience similar enlightenment? Here are stories of a couple of my "fights" and my growth as a result.

Healthy Options and the Right to Choose

An error does not become truth by reason of multiplied propaga-
tion, nor does truth become error because nobody sees it.
                                              —Mohandas Gandhi

It's an interesting life dynamic to walk your talk, but how far do you take it? I asked myself that question when living in a conservative and somewhat elite town for nearly 15 years. I will say upfront that I have a good life, I just find myself doing a bit of a balancing act, at times, to figure out why folks aren't "seeing" certain things. We all have "no way, really?" or "ah ha" moments that catapult us into doing something bigger than ourselves. It doesn't happen everyday thank goodness or we'd never get daily chores done, but when it does, watch out.

One of my "no way, really?" moments happened when I found out the truth about what our schools across the US offered our children as "nutrition." My initial wake up came when watching the documentary, "Super Size Me." It talked about specific fast food chain trends, but even more importantly to me, at the time, was the realization that many schools support bad snack habits in the name of profit for their food service departments. When cornered, schools defend their "extra profit offers" by deferring to the balanced meals that are offered by the national school lunch programs funded by their state. And when the less healthy food is chosen, they say the children make the bad choices. I don't know about you, but when I have candy and cookies in the house, I have been known to eat them! So what do we do to partake less? We don't bring them into our houses!

When I began bringing data to parents' attention, what surprised me is that most weren't shocked and, in fact, didn't even care—even when I shared that our local school (in central Ohio) sold nearly 150,000 candy bars to our middle and high school students in a school year (2003/2004), 110,000 artificial and sugared drinks, and over 33,000 fast food pizzas were offered. It seemed like our middle and high schools were creating convenience stores in our school cafeterias. And as an introduction of things to come to the wannabe teens, a freestanding sweet cart was offered in elementary school during lunch.

When I went to the Board of Education and Superintendent and asked, "Why are we serving junk to our kids?" I was met with apathy and was pushed back with praise for the food service manager. My research revealed that the "a la carte" junk food and drinks equated to approximately $350,000 in profit, so it made perfect business sense.

Even more ludicrous, I was turned away by the Board of Education saying that taking these items out of the mix would *create a violation of children's rights to choose.* And to cover their tracks even further, food service management later put green, yellow and red tags on all the snack items. An article on "colored snack tags" even hit the suburban newspapers and was positioned like an answer to parents' concerns on bad food choice offerings in our school cafeteria's. Then when the children picked up the red dotted items (meaning bad choice) they could (again) pass the blame onto the kids and parents. So like the smoking (sin) tax funding healthcare in the United States, sugar profit was helping our food service department create a cost effective department.

So how could I respond in love? How could I be firm, yet open-minded? Here's what printed in a "Letter to the Editor" in our suburban paper.

Schools need to reevaluate its junk food offerings

To the Editor:

This is in response to 'District hopes snack labels will help with better choices.' While I am working with (the school) administration (as a concerned parent) to try and change the offerings in our school cafeterias, I'm not sure why professionals trained in nutrition experienced "open(ed) eyes" when attempting to execute this new labeling program.

We are literally selling hundreds of thousands of candy bars alone in our middle and high schools. Do we really need signage on Reeses cups and chocolate bars? When I approached the School Board in the fall, the majority deemed the junk food offerings a non-issue. The School Board President went as far as to say that if we don't offer junk we would have issues with district parents because kids' rights to choose would be violated, plus our food service department is self-supporting as a result (so what's the problem with a few poor choices/sugar profit?).

More and more credible studies (that we already knew to be true intuitively) are being shared linking higher test scores and better behavior to better quality food intake.

Parents of the School District, don't take my word for it. Walk into middle or high school cafeterias, observe what our kids are purchasing.

It's not a perfect world; we all like junk treats now and then but why not educate by providing good choices (meaning Reeses cups would not show up on food service purchase orders)? Then when our kids are on their own, they might gravitate to the good things they've experimented with at (our) schools. Talk about a great way to educate: Leading by example!

Michelle Payton

(Published in OLENTANGY VALLEY NEWS, Letter to the Editor, March 30, 2005)

Well, the gauntlet had been dropped numerous times and it wasn't about to stop now. The following week we heard from the "other side."

Parental role is key issue in childhood diet debate

To the Editor:

The following is in response to the recent letter, 'Schools need to reevaluate its junk food offerings.' While the letter writer, Ms. Payton, and I will disagree on the definition of a proper diet—I prefer raw oatmeal and apple juice for breakfast over more standard fare—the real issue here is the role of parents versus the role of pressure groups and government: in this case your local school board.

The facts: The. . . school district provides what are considered to be nutritious meals. I use the qualifier "considered" simply because we don't serve the raw oatmeal which I attribute to good health nor do we serve the exact diet that Ms. Payton assumes best.

We do though serve balanced meals that exceed federal standards. In addition, we provide the opportunity for students to vary their meals through a la carte menu selections, or, to opt out and pack a lunch of their choice.

Through our district-issued lunch debit card, we also provide parents with the means to limit and monitor their children's food purchases. Under the district's current food service program, all parents have the ability to guarantee that their children eat a nutritious diet.

The issue: Who gets control over your children? Is it a vocal pressure group or you, the parent? Haven't we all heard from those who claim to be concerned about our children? Pressure groups use this line of argument to entice government to force parents to adhere to the groups' standards.

Similar diet advocates aren't satisfied by modifications to lunch and vending machine offerings, they also want to limit that which can be packed in the brown bag and lunch box along with that which can be served during class parties.

These advocates always know best and they work to force school boards to bend to their will. Out goes reason and parental rights and in comes additional government controls over your lives. Today the issue is diet, tomorrow it will be something else.

What is the proper role of the school board? Is it to engage in the latest form of social engineering by bending to the voice of vocal pressure groups and mandating parental decisions, or is it simply to provide cost-effective programs that meet our mission statement?

If it is the latter, we are working to achieve that goal. If it is the former, watch out for the raw oatmeal and apple juice that I will be serving.

Member Board of Education

(Published in OLENTANGY VALLEY NEWS, Letter to the Editor, April 6, 2005)

Hmmmm... Call me psychic, but I'm pretty sure that this Board of Education member didn't buy into the idea of better quality food in our school cafeterias.

So why am I sharing this?

1. This is a nationwide issue in America's public school systems, which has also contributed to the demise of overall health in the United States beyond school.

2. America in the early 2000's is the fattest country in the world and physical inactivity and nutrition-related diseases have become one of the leading causes of preventable death.

3. Children spend approximately one-third of their day in school. Ensuring schools provide appropriate food is one of the keys to our children's success to help them perform at optimal levels academically and in life.

4. We are not going to be popular when we work to move the needle on an idea larger than we are and it can be a challenge to balance opinions with respect, honor, integrity and love.

5. Our life challenge is to keep our enlightened heads—to believe in ourselves and our internal guidance while addressing the issue completely so as to effectively move the needle. Breaking destructive

patterns for more than just you and your loved ones creates healing at a global level and benefits the ALL IS ONE.

So I pulled (or so I thought) the "I'm going over your head" tactic and went to the Ohio Board of Education. It turned out that they had little influence on any local school district in regards to "a la carte" snacks. Back down the ladder, I collected solid data with the help of the food service department. (Yep, you heard me right. They were required to give me reports.) Up another ladder, I approached the House of Representatives and Senate in Columbus, Ohio to potentially draw up a bill. With the suggestion of our local House of Representatives, I collected information on what other states were executing and contacted the senator in California sponsoring the "School Nutrition Bill" and the Texas Department of Agriculture that had executed a comprehensive nutrition policy to limit bad food in their school systems. I'm not sure what ladder this would be, but for good measure, I sent a report to every Parent Teacher Organization in our school district (14 at that time) to increase awareness and provide accurate data.

By the time the House of Representatives aide called me and thanked me for the detailed package I sent them, the budgets (which included school money allocations) were their priority. They would consider taking a closer look at the matter in the summer. Patience was the key.

Throughout this process, some of the more difficult challenges were: keeping my ego in check each time I felt rejected, insulted, or frustrated due to the lack of support (because an organization or individual couldn't or wouldn't help); and letting go of things I just didn't have control over. Numerous phone calls, face-to-face meetings and crunched numbers later, I provided data to all that could possibly move the effort forward. I was worn down, for my emotional and physical well being I had to let go to the next level and let the Universe run with this. After seven months, others had to grab the baton and run with it.

This was my parting message to the local newspapers and email to interested friends.

SUBJECT: HOUSE OF REPRESENTATIVES CONSIDERING DRAFTING BILL ON SNACKS SERVED IN SCHOOL CAFETERIAS

I am a mother of three living in the . . . School District and felt it important to provide data to other parents in regards to our school system offering an overabundance of "empty calorie" snacks in our school cafeterias to keep the Food Service Department cost-effective. After many months of research and contacting numerous committees and agencies, (House of) Representative Peterson is considering sponsoring a bill to support children's health in relation to school cafeteria snack offerings. When receiving my initial packet of information on what our specific school offers, he requested more research on what other states were doing and I forwarded the Senate Bill #12 currently being discussed in California and what the State of Texas (Department of Agriculture) has executed in its schools.

Be clear that when/if the Food Service Department changes its strategy to provide more healthy snack choices for our students, they are not fulfilling their job requirements to "create cost-effective programs" in accordance with the Board of Education mission since . . .Food Service is generating over $285,000 per year retail sales in candy and sugared drinks alone. And this doesn't end with our school district. This is a nationwide problem of balancing our children's health with making profit. Here are some facts:

1. While school districts are quick to quote their National School Lunch program offerings (technically, the well-balanced meal offering) and clean facilities awards, and assuming that the . . .Food Service Department's estimates are correct—less than half of our middle school and less than 30% of our high school students participate in this program. That assumption being correct, then

2. When/if the School District STOPS selling candy bars (peanut butter cups, chocolate bars, Nestle Crunch, Kit Kat and the like), they will suffer a loss of OVER $100,000 (per year/annum) in gross (retail) income! Our school district sold over 148,000 candy bars of ten varieties to (predominantly) our middle and high school students in 2003/2004 school year. That is over 830 candy bars per school day!

3. Artificial flavor drinks of three varieties—Yoohoo (20g sugar, 29g carbohydrates), Fruit Craze (10% fruit juice and 15g sugar, 15g carbohydrates), Gatorade (14g sugar, 14g carbohydrates to restore electrolytes in athletes when working out)—bring our school system over $150,000 per year in gross retail income! This is over 109,000 sugar drinks of only three varieties!

4. One of . . . (the) School district's top selling entrée's is pizza. 19% of our total student sales are fast food pizza from Donatos and Papa Johns (approximately 33,000 units of pizza). While not necessarily a realistic option to wipe off the menu, it reveals a less healthy purchase pattern with approximately $250,000 to $300,000 in gross (retail) income or 32,981 Papa John's and Donato's pizza's sold during 2003/2004 (estimated gross dollars from $206,133 wholesale purchases). Grouped with candy and sugared drinks, a school meal has little to no nutritional value.

5. Many items, including potato chips, ice cream, muffins and the like could not be calculated due to incomplete information.

We all like treats now and then and if parents want their children to have these types of snacks, they can certainly send them from home. But shouldn't (the school) . . .and all other school districts be held accountable for making hundreds of thousands of dollars at the risk of our children's health and classroom performance? I'm happy to field further questions for which I have data, but like CA, TX and other districts, I'm holding the vision that our local government will soon draft a bill. . . to help our school system, as well as others, do what's healthiest for our children since no other agencies, boards, departments or committees have had the will or simply the ability to do the right thing.

There. I said it. I did my job. Or so I thought.

Have you ever been embarrassed by opposition? Have you ever attempted to embarrass the opposition? How did embarrassment feel with each situation? What if you're not being heard? How does that feel? When have you shut others out? How did that work out?

Doing Your Best Then Bowing Out Gracefully

Honest disagreement is often a good sign of progress.
—Mohandas Gandhi

Letting go doesn't mean that you no longer care, it simply means you've done everything you can at that moment in time and it's simply time to allow the Universe to take its course. This is what I had to finally do with the food issue in my school system after I shared the data with school organizations, parents and local media. I took a step back and reminded myself that this was about changing destructive patterns. The patterns that required reprogramming included:

Redirecting school administrators goals so that they no longer viewed financial gain as more important than our children's health (in the school cafeterias);

Reminding school administrators that they were creating problems for our children during school hours (and beyond) as they were, literally, physically handicapping our children in the classroom (performance, focus, behavior…) when providing an overabundance of carbohydrates, fat and sugar options to our children;

Training our children to know that adults aren't always educated enough in certain subjects to maintain health. It also takes initiative from them.

I talked about brain development at the beginning of this book. Young people view themselves as invincible, and have a difficult time connecting with the concept of long-term effects. When kids are offered vegetables and a candy bar as "food offerings," while the kids might know the difference they don't fully believe there are consequences to their bodies and their performances in the classroom (highs and lows, lethargy, upset stomach, physical body shakes...). And let's face it, a lot of the adult population battle similar issues.

These issues became too consuming for me, and (I perceived) didn't seem to matter to the masses. As soon as I let go, the local paper called and asked for my input on an article on the cafeteria food issue. This is what it said:

Resident Wants District and State To Limit Food Choices

Powell resident Michelle Payton is taking her fight to reduce the amount of sugar and fat in student lunches to the Statehouse.

Whether she will be successful in her attempts to limit food choices in the state's lunchrooms remains to be seen.

For several months, Payton has been working with the office of state Rep. Jon Peterson (R-Delaware) to develop stricter standards for the fare offered in cafeterias. The move is a continuation of a battle that began last year when Payton approached the... Local School District, asking it to reduce the availability of candy bars and certain soft drinks in schools.

Payton said she is upset that students are taught about healthful choices in health classes, then sent to a cafeteria that serves Papa John's pizza and Yoohoo soft drinks.

"This is a learning environment," Payton said. 'This is a training ground.'

"Bad food choices can affect the learning environment," Payton said.

"What happens when children can't overcome temptations? Then, other children suffer because they can't overcome the sugar high," she said.

So far, officials have not been quick to act. Although Peterson and ... school board members and administrators have said they do their best to offer healthful alternatives, they are in no rush to eliminate items from school menus.

"We would rather look at education and increasing physical activity among students," said Peterson. "There is some reservation in the House about prohibiting certain foods at school."

School board member ... believes Payton is overstepping boundaries.

"This is somebody who wants to stick her nose into purely parental decisions," he said. "Her problem is not with her children, it's with everybody elses'."

"The district offers a broad menu with many nutritional choices, including meals conforming to the US Department of Agriculture's 'Type A' lunch standards," . . .the board member wrote—"More regulation is not necessary."

"The issue is parental choice," he said. "We serve a meal that's balanced according to federal standards. Michelle Payton has an opinion and that's fine—using an arm of government to enforce it on others is inappropriate."

(The) food service director . . . said narrowing selection in the district's cafeteria is not necessary since parents already have the option of blocking certain items from the debit cards used by students in the cafeteria.

Payton said that is not sufficient. "Some parents have said when they do put blocks on their children's cards, their kids get very angry with them," Payton said. "Why put this in front of our children? When we don't want to be tempted in our own households, we don't bring in cookies and candy bars."

"My biggest concern is that (the school district) sells approximately 150,000 candy bars to our middle and high schoolers (each year). . ."

. . .officials said they are constantly reviewing their menus and are willing to consider all suggestions, although it is unlikely such changes will be made in the district's lunchrooms.

Peterson said he hopes to introduce a bill setting guidelines relating to student health and activity, but he is not likely to include Payton's prohibitions in the bill.

(Published in OLENTANGY VALLEY NEWS, By Mark Major, June 6, 2005)

The local school board member was getting a bit personal and when my oldest read this article she said, "Mom, he 'dogged' you!" But my perception was that this was more of a negative energy that this official had created for himself—and an unexpected development resulted. A number of parents shared that they were very offended that a parent was criticized so harshly by an elected school official. This was the turning point that made this bigger to other parents (an individual saying, "What if I did something like this? Would I be treated so negatively?"). One parent said she wrote to this official saying I deserved nothing less than a public apology and the school (where she worked) was buzzing about this issue (the cafeteria food AND the public official comments). It brought to mind a Buddhist saying to which I feel a strong connection to (and summarize in my own mainstream metaphysical words): "At my last breath, the only thing I truly have is my actions and the grace in which I've handled myself day-to-day which gives me more peaceful moments in my lifetime." It was clear that I had not "persuaded" the local school district to make any changes. The Ohio House of Representatives and Senate didn't take a hard line, either. I did my best—sometimes with grace, other times with struggle (depending on whose eyes you're looking through).

When have you struggled with handling something gracefully? Why? When did you handle a tough situation gracefully? How can you duplicate grace?

A Rebel Tired of the Cause

I claim to be a simple individual liable to err like any other fellow mortal. I own, however, that I have humility enough to confess my errors and to retrace my steps.

—Mohandas Gandhi

In my past books, I have made the broad brush statement (conceptually) that some of my thoughts will hit home for you and others may not. When I've been interviewed by various media, I have been told by some,

"You seem to contradict yourself." My response is "Haven't you changed day to day?" Because I've changed my mind, does it mean that what I've said in the past is no longer true for someone else? We develop in stages and we don't all go through the same stages.

I reserve the right to be in that ever changing space. So when I continued down this track of "healthy choices" in our school cafeterias I became more and more uncomfortable. Why? Because I was now requesting the House of Representatives and Senate of Ohio to turn certain suggestions into law.

A rider was put on the budget bill that included a Wellness Council. This energy ball was getting much bigger. One week later, one of the local television stations gave me a ring, "Are you Michelle Payton, the parent that helped push the Wellness Council through the House of Representatives?" My answer, "Yes, I am Michelle Payton. No, I am not responsible for the rider put on a house bill called the Wellness Council." I supported the Wellness Council concept, but believed that the guidelines wouldn't be followed unless it's connected to money (someone or something would have to replace the income generated by candy bars, sugared drinks and the like). Taking a little wind out of this journalist's story, the newscaster and video crew still showed up at my house to interview me. They also went to the school lunchrooms to get footage on what kids are purchasing at lunchtime. When she asked me "Why are you doing this?" All of a sudden, I drew a blank. Why was I forcing my opinions on everyone else? My kids ate healthy. Our family was fit and conscious. Even my then 4-year-old knew the difference between a protein source and a carbohydrate. Why was I putting myself so far out into the mainstream community? Was this a good use of my time?

At that very moment I was ready to say, "I don't know." But, that wouldn't be newsworthy, would it? The story that ran on our local television station included a visual and verbal of me saying "the system is definitely flawed." They showed junk food in the schools and even in their studios they talked about diets gone bad. It had become a cause that I was tired of leading, and I simply stopped.

Since that time—even after moving from Ohio—I've heard from different women on a couple of occasions in that school district. My response, in a nutshell, has been, "this is not a polite exchange and takes a lot of focus." There is no such thing as politically correct when proposing change.

When have you put your heart into something and realized that it was time to step away? How did you detach? When is detaching the right decision with any particular situation?

Integrative Medicine and Practices in a Mainstream Pharmaceutical Country

Every human being is the author of his own health or disease.
—Buddha

If the availability of healthy food choices was a controversial subject, imagine the uproar if integrative medicine was discussed! A TV newscaster said one morning as a headline, "Warning even though H1N1 is not an issue right now it's important you get your shot." The underlying extension to the message was "because pharmaceutical company shareholders are upset that their stock values have gone down."

When I was pregnant with my third child, my mainstream doctor recommended that I take a multi-vitamin that she could prescribe and was covered by insurance. It was pharmaceutically produced as opposed to cold pressed or naturally grown like a whole food, which meant that it would be difficult to digest if at all. I advised my obstetrician that I would be taking a supplement that was better for me and my baby in development and left it at that.

Many medical schools are now including information on complementary and alternative medicine to focus on overall health of the mind, body and spirit. Hypnotherapy is credible enough to be used in courts of law in certain states, and is used by many in the medical professional, and it has a great deal of research supporting its effectiveness. But mainstream minds do still close. For instance, while chiropractic work was introduced in the US in 1895, a former pediatrician (for my children) insisted that I was harming my children by allowing my family to be treated.

Preventative medicine is hugely untapped—with the exception of immunizations. For some fatal diseases, immunizations have been helpful. However we don't always know what is being injected into ours or our children's bodies, and mistakes are made. For instance, a booster gone wrong, in 1955 Cutter Laboratories failed to kill the polio in 120,000 doses of the vaccines and forty thousand people contracted a strand of the polio virus after receiving the vaccine. About 56 were paralyzed due to the illness and 5 children died. (http://en.wikipedia.org/wiki/Cutter_Laboratories.) In the 1980's the same lab (purchased by Bayer, who makes aspirin, in the 1970's) created unsafe blood products to treat hemophilia. The product was contaminated with HIV.

So are we excessively immunizing and medicating? What about more natural ways to protect our population? We know that children who are breast milk fed are protected from certain diseases. Florence Nightingale saved lives (and still does due to her research and fortitude) by increasing good hygiene practices in hospitals (I am still amazed when I see grown adults walk out of public rest rooms without washing their hands). Hundreds of thousands contract sexually transmitted diseases which shorten lives even after treated, but became preventable with simple safety practices. While Kosher preparation is considered more of a spiritual practice by many, there are sanitary practices that ultimately maintained health among the Jewish population. What else can we do? My youngest (born in 2001) received her whooping cough booster as "recommended" and still contracted this condition in 2008. Some may say, "It was likely less severe as a result of having the immunization," but where is that controlled study? Is it always about taking a pill or a shot?

The chicken pox virus shot had become all the rage by the early 2000's. I was regularly reminded when I took my youngest to the pediatrician, about this inoculation. I refused over and over again, and they insisted I sign papers stating that I opted out, but continued on their path of spouting off insignificant and misleading mortality statistics. My research revealed, however, chicken pox was not the cause of death, but the complications of additional conditions like pneumonia, other infections and treatments by doctors. Even the Center for Disease Control admits that children don't die from chicken pox. Regardless of receiving the vaccine, like we experienced first hand with the whooping cough, she would still be susceptible to the chicken pox and its cousin, shingles.

Ironically, around the same time, my high school girl was being advised to take the human papillomavirus or HPV shot (recommended for girls' ages 11 or earlier to 26-years-old). According to www.gardasil.com, the Human papillomaviruses (HPV) are common viruses that can cause warts. Most are harmless, but about 30 types put you at risk for cancer. These types affect the genitals and you get them through sexual contact with an infected partner causing a low-risk HPV of genital warts and "sometimes" can create a high risk HPV of cancers of the cervix, vulva, vagina and anus in women. In men, it can lead to cancers of the anus and penis. I gave my high school girl the option, she opted-out.

But just because I've written this is in black and white, don't take my word for it. Do your own research on all "recommendations" for you and your family. You'll be glad you took the time.

So my layman's view has become that some immunizations are over the top. In the same breath, I will say there are some good things that have come from immunizing. It is recommended, for instance, not to immunize if a child is sick. If their immune systems are down then there are risks of more adverse reactions occurring. Then there is also a school of thought floating around that 80–90% of infection will be resistant to all known antibiotics! What do we do with that? Kill, not just some, but all of the bacteria in our intestines (like chemotherapy) then use another drug to add all the good bacteria —current holistic procedure is to consume probiotics to bring good bacteria count back up, but what will it be tomorrow? And not just everyday Jane's are taking a step back. In 1998, France became the first country to stop requiring the hepatitis B vaccine due to numerous reports of children developing chronic arthritis and symptoms of Multiple Sclerosis following the vaccine.

Mainstream pharmaceuticals have taken a stab at preventative medicine with some success. However inadequate (sometimes careless) chemical mixtures, immunizations with overzealous claims to create rather than serve needs, and marketers treating inoculations like packaged goods to serve up "what's next" to please shareholders, are losing their way. There are books, books and more good books on natural or home remedies (all easy to research on the Internet)—wonder herbs like nettle to reduce allergic reactions, full of vitamins and minerals for hormonal balance and more. There's apple cider vinegar (in lieu of many pharmaceuticals) for colds, coughs, bone health, digestion and heartburn issues and many other remedies; hydrogen peroxide or garlic for ear infections (in lieu of antibiotics); sea salt water nose rinses for allergies and congestion and more. Look for the balance.

Consider tracking cyclical health challenges in your household, then gather natural remedy recipes to arm yourself, for instance, for allergies, coughs and colds, indigestion, stomach upset, hormone balancing, and ear infections. Empower yourself.

When is it Time to Live our Lives? What Tools Can We Use to Define "Live?"

Do not dwell in the past, do not dream of the future, concentrate the mind on the present moment. —Buddha

There is health and then there is the absolute change. They put him in his chair and found him slumped over an hour later... Gone... She was found dressed for the day, she took her last breath and had just fallen gracefully back onto her bed. ...She died peacefully in her sleep. ...He went with family surrounding him, nothing left unsaid.

Nearly all of us have in common a vision of an easy passage when leaving our bodies—Peaceful, Graceful, Loving, Comfortable, Quick. The question is, "How do we live our lives using these similar positive descriptors?"

I just finished receiving a massage and said, "I am really getting my heart rate up with all the things that need to be done for the kids at the end of the school year." The enviable response I received was, "I don't get caught up in all that." My respectful response, "No kids or are they grown?" At that time, I was caring for elementary, middle school and high school aged kids—all completely different development stages. My husband had always done more than his fair share when he was in town, but it could be really chaotic at times. To calm myself, I wrote down goals on how to do life with more grace while other activity swirled around me. I asked:

1. What am I looking forward to? I have a number of new places to visit, books to write, hobbies to adopt, yoga poses to learn and perfect, tea chats to have, family events to enjoy, kids to watch grow/expand… What excited me about life? This included applying my F.I.P.S.S—Financial, Intellectual, Physical, Social, Spiritual—process to create comfort (see my book *"Soul"utions* for more details on this process).

2. How many buttons should I push then let go? Once I put a dream on paper, I was working toward something. Then I put ample effort— researched, looked at financial, intellectual, physical, social, spiritual implications, got buy-in from my life partner—into tightening up my thoughts to state realistic goals. It was like adding ingredients to soup and then letting it simmer. There's an art to how much pushing (researching, discussing, strategizing) and when to let go. We rarely get this right, but the two concepts—push and let go—are two of the key components to effort meeting Universal buy-in. So after letting go, energy runs its natural course. And, many times, letting go runs in intervals or rest periods—let go, push forward, let go, push forward. There's physical feeling you may get when it's time to put the brakes on—sometimes overwhelm, sometimes doubt, sometimes you know you've done enough for the time being, sometimes you get pushed back because you are shoving too hard.

3. If I'm planning so much, how do I realize the joy in the moment? While I wrote this I was on a ten hour driving trip with my family. I sat

in the back seat of my van with my teen daughter's legs sprawled on me during parts of the trip, her head on my lap other times, and she even held my hand at one point without my prompting. My other two played video games and read. My preschooler (at the time) handed me a book now and again to read to her as she sucked her thumb. My mom (also traveling with us) barely took a breath as she continually talked to my husband while he was driving. We were stuck with each other. The joy of the moment and the mental snap shot was complete when my youngest turned to face me in the back seat, gave me a big smile, a wave, and said "I love you Mommy." And I heard the words: Peaceful; Graceful; Loving; Comfortable.

How do you balance long-term and short-term thinking? Think of examples of when you did both and what kind of success you experienced? Think of examples when you could only think short or long-term, what kind of success did you experience? Have you considered that sometimes the long-term goal is to think short-term or the short-term goal is to think long-term? Or, is it all about being in the moment?

V. Following-Through and Conscious Thinking

Even death is not to be feared by one who has lived wisely.

—Buddha

E ven with all the noise connected to financial, intellectual, social, spiritual and physical endeavors, enlightenment is achievable while living in the mainstream world. Achievement is where intuitive and intellectual effort meets the flow of synchronicity, where there is subconscious and conscious agreement. So this section is dedicated to problem/solution, cause/effect, hitting targets, the "ah ha" moments, and the little things that turn out (many times unbeknownst at the time) to have lasting life effects.

Follow-through is one of the biggest issues needing attention for myself, my family, and the people I work with. Understanding when effectively using the mind as a tool is empowering. Pick and choose how the following random snippets fit for you.

Guided Follow-Through as a Child

Everyone who wills can hear the inner voice. It is within every-
one.   —Mohandas Gandhi

My mother said that I was called "little grandma" as early as one-year-old. When I was about 7-years-old (first grade), a dentist came into our classroom. He brought a big model mouth with teeth, a giant toothbrush, kid size toothbrushes and toothpaste, and little red pills that (when after being chewed) showed how poorly you brushed your teeth. The dentist demonstrated how to properly brush our teeth using his giant model, then he gave us our toothbrushes and toothpaste and we all brushed our teeth. Then we sucked on the little red pill and looked in our mouths and witnessed the bad job we did brushing and then we brushed them all over again. So why is this story significant?

My father was an alcoholic and drug abuser so household money disappeared at times to cover the basics. At this particular time we didn't have running water in our house because the utility bill wasn't paid. These were the days before bottled water was sold like soda, but there was a condemned home in the area that (oddly enough) did have running water. So I filled a bowl with water from the tap of the deserted home to brush my teeth until our utilities were restored.

When I look at my and other children I wonder, where did I get that idea? Where did I get that drive? There were rats running around in this building and it was frightening, why would I be so brave at such a young age? Why did I follow through?

In the area where I lived, many people's teeth were uncared for. Images of black stumps where there once were white teeth, puffy red gums, and worse were commonplace. By the time my mother was in her thirties her teeth were disintegrating before my young eyes. Once we had dental insurance for a short stint (when I was in middle/junior high school), she had them all pulled and replaced with dentures. Now (as I write) in my late 40's, my teeth have been one of my personal signs of successful passage into adulthood. And keeping my natural teeth has been even more important. My three children have also benefited as none of them have cavities—ages 19, 17 and 9 at the moment of writing this passage.

What encouraged me to break from that pattern? What encourages you to break from patterns? We naturally move toward our highest goods, so what allows us to hear, see, and feel the healthiest directions?

When It's Clear that Others Want to See You Fail and Bitter Pill Follow-Through

In the practice of tolerance, one's enemy is the best teacher.

—Dalai Lama

Even as we push ourselves toward success, knowingly or maybe not so obviously, we've all been in situations where people truly want to see us fail. It's as simple as when you're a child and your sibling(s) wanted to see you get in trouble, when you've played sports and spectators in the stands or on the other team encourage you to miss plays, or when someone starts laughing when they see you drop and break something. Some people are just angry at the world and want to project that on anyone that crosses their paths, and the list goes on and on. And this type of "wishful thinking" creates a super accelerated failure energy that can sometimes be impossible to overcome unless you simply pull yourself entirely out of the situation.

There was a time in my corporate professional life where I walked into a hornets' nest as a new hire. I was in my thirties, I had two preschool aged children, I was driving about 100 miles per day to get to and from work so my husband shouldered a lot of the responsibility to take care of our children. This was a great growth opportunity—great job and good money. That is, until the first day I sat down at my new desk. To set the stage, I was hired by a director that few of my peers and above liked or respected. And most of my brand management peers and above would do anything to prove that this guy should not be in the marketing department. Many of the group, that reported to the other director, were outwardly rude and clearly interested in seeing me fail to prove (yet again) that the director I reported to was not qualified to be there (Note: All of my peers and above also interviewed me, so I was obviously a good fit). In the first week, even if I'd asked where the bathroom was, they'd point me in the wrong direction.

Ultimately, they were successful in eliminating him, and in less than two years I reported to three different people, and two of those were promoted rude peers. I was living a nearly 2-year nightmare professionally. I inherited a poorly managed budget mid-fiscal year where all expenditures were already overcommitted by my predecessor, and for which I was blamed for the shortfall at the end of the fiscal year. I was being (literally) screamed at by the other director in public who, once my old manager was eliminated, humiliated *me* numerous times. The politics were so heavy that I had to plead to get a major company wide presentation approved by the marketing vice president just days prior to a sales meeting. Then I was forced to change the presentation in between meetings (due to newly emerged politics at the company wide kickoff), which ruined my chances of being an effective marketer for this company. Following that fiasco, a sales manager that I connected with called me from the field saying "I want to brainstorm with you on some marketing ideas before the company totally beats you down." If I made MY OWN mistakes (and I did), it was tenfold recognized and gossiped about. But what was clear to everyone was that I was easy to get along with, enjoyed people, was creative, and loved my line of work. The politics, however, were just insurmountable from the minute I accepted the position. There was no one watching my back.

I was so relieved to have the freedom to walk out those doors for good—so much that I shed tears of joy. Here's the biggest point of my story. Follow-through comes in many forms. Regardless of who is responsible, failure (yours or others) allows us to fully and consciously connect to situations so that we can heal. And leaving an unchangeable or dysfunctional situation, regardless of who owns what responsibility, is the healthiest follow-through.

Are there situations or people that aren't serving your highest good? What change is the healthiest for you?

What You Want in Life using Conscious and Subconscious Follow-Through

However many holy words you read, however many you speak,
what good will they do you if you do not act (on upon) them?
—Buddha

The interesting thing about intentions is they manifest in exactly the way you think. You can outwardly word intentions in a way that would seem to manifest your desire, but if your thinking doesn't match then it's a "no go." The conscious and subconscious minds must agree to serve you completely.

So what is an intention? It's ultimately an achievement that you've followed-through on. You have a desire, you put a plan in place, and then something has manifested as a result of actions taken.

So how are we all doing on manifesting?

What if your intention is to lose weight?

If someone says "I'm watching what I eat," what is this person accomplishing? Literally, this person is achieving watching what she eats. This can be watched in large volumes or small volumes, consuming healthy or junk food. How about "I am eating healthy food and continue to achieve and maintain my optimal weight." You could also add a "how much" and "by when" statement like "Now I am consuming the right amount of fruit, vegetables, protein, fiber and water to maintain the healthiest weight for me."

What if someone wants to have more money?

If someone says "I'm managing my debt" or worse, "I'm trying to get out of debt" what is this person accomplishing? Literally, this person is monkeying around with his/her debt instead of creating cash flow, and the second statement says he/she is spending his/her time trying to get out of debt. How about "My cash flow is allowing me to travel to..., purchase a..., save..., invest..., pay for college...," and have a solid "how much" money and "by when" statement.

What if someone's intention is to have a positive romantic relationship?

If someone says "I'm no longer dating lazy, unsuccessful, losers" then his/her focus on lazy, unsuccessful, losers will be his/her focus. How about "I am dating a successful, healthy, energetic, winner," and make sure you add "now" to that statement.

Write one or two intentions. Does what you're saying "feel" comfortable? Wordsmith your intentions so both minds agree (you won't hear doubts or arguments in your mind). If you feel comfortable, ask someone else to read your intentions. This will get you closer to achieving.

Quieting the Mind using Self-Hypnosis Follow-Through

Peace comes from within. Do not seek it without. —Buddha

To get clarity on situations you want in your life, sometimes it's important to get into a quiet space. I did a seminar on self-hypnosis and a listener asked if by quieting our minds or stopping thought was, over time, limiting our creative thought process or just redirecting it?

The answer is that we're not stopping thought. Stopping thought in our mind and body means our physical bodies no longer function. What we are doing is relaxing and freeing our mind and body.

Why does this benefit you? If you're interested in increasing your ability to focus, hear, listen, receive, create, and relax more easily, this is a great self-help, mind over matter tool for you. Other perks include good overall health and harmony for you and everyone that surrounds you.

For instance, think about a time when you were on a simple mission, like walking into a room to retrieve something and you forgot why you were going to that room, or when you were in the middle of a thought and forgot where you were going with it, or you forgot someone's name or the proper name of something. Be clear that this is completely normal, because our thoughts are constantly firing off in multiple directions. It's once you quiet the mind that answers pop into your head like, what seems like, magic. Maybe this has happened to you, hours before you couldn't think of someone's name then it pop's into your head, almost like the information was just lined up in a cue and, finally, it was that answer's turn.

What would be alarming is if you were walking toward a room and you forgot where you were, or when you were in the middle of a discussion and you no longer recognized to whom you were talking.

Let's get a quick grasp on accessing information in that all knowing mind of ours. First you should know that you've experienced trance states a number of times already today, yesterday, last week, last month. For example:

- When you began to wake up today
- When you took a shower or bath
- Blow drying your hair
- Listening to the radio or watching TV
- Reading the newspaper
- Reading a book (like now)
- Driving to work or another destination
- Listening to the radio while driving
- Doing some light body stretching work
- Taking a few deep breaths
- Taking a walk or running in silence
- Taking a walk or running listening to music
- Working out at the gym with or without music
- Participating in an aerobics class
- Participating in a yoga class
- Participating in a sporting activity
- Playing an instrument
- Painting
- Drawing
- Beginning to go to sleep

- Meditating
- Closing your eyes with deep breathing
- Listening to a lecture (not writing)
- Watching a movie—in a theatre its like a group trance and you are so connected you laugh, cry, and get angry while listening and consequently experiencing the movie

With any of these you can lose a sense of time and space. You've jumped into your own little world. You are completely in that moment of being or experiencing. It's those times when someone has to call your name several times before you are aware that they are talking to you. Some call this "being in the zone."

When in this space you are in more of a right brain mode, a receiving, imagining, artful, creating mode. For instance, if you begin to write while listening, the left side of your brain is accessed. Your left and right brain cannot work at the same time (although they can have different switching speeds). So if you are one of those people that begins to write and then you get into a rut because you are frustrated that you can't seem to comprehend the material at that moment, patience is the key. Take a recorder if you are in a classroom experience so you can transcribe while in class, then relisten outside of class. When you respect this physiological fact, your absorption of material reaches approximately 90%.

Here's an assignment to be able to take advantage during these relaxed states just mentioned. Connect to several of the moments to understand how it feels to your body, mind, and spirit. The more you understand how you "wear" that peace, that mind state, that waking trance state, the more you can use this as a clarity and relaxation tool.

Getting to a Happy Place with
Childish Follow-Through

The purpose of our lives is to be happy.   —Dalai Lama

What if you can't seem to relax? Stress and the dis-ease that follows is all about the constant emotional blows that then impact the physical body. To search for origins of stress, many times in hypnotherapy I take people back as far as they need to go to remember why they are stressed. Sounds odd, but we forget, or rather our minds block information to protect ourselves and then we limp emotionally forward in attempts to do life as functionally as possible.

For instance, right now you are reading and receiving information and this automatically puts you in a relaxed state or waking trance state (unless you disagree with the information and you are developing inner chatter). If I suggest that right now you go back to an extremely happy moment during childhood, you could immediately visualize one of your joyful memories.

Then, if I ask you about the weather during this experience and how it feels on your physical body, the smells, the sights, the sounds, and even the tastes, you are connecting to the stored memories of your subconscious mind.

So congratulations, you just did a short self-hypnosis exercise to create relaxation.

This simple exercise is helpful to you like regularly doing weight training or exercising. Bonus: when you spend time visualizing you actually improve your overall ability to remember the small stuff. Practicing something so simple and happy, you begin to know how you "wear" relaxation and happiness using easy trance states. You have reignited a place to freely access your subconscious. Naturally.

Clarifying Intentions with Relaxed State Follow-Through

Action expresses priorities.   —Mohandas Gandhi

So in the relaxed zones that you create for yourself, you can also set intentions. This may be for the purpose of getting answers, putting plans in motion once you have access to your subconscious or just to relax to create good physical health.

So before you jump into your zone, state your purpose and, after you've completed your activity, restate your intention. If you have a question, state it before your activity to the point of literal silliness. "To my subconsious mind and the Universal energy, any that are there to help me achieve success, please provide me an answer to..." When you have completed your activity, state that "your mind is open and ready to receive an answer to..." Some information may have occurred to you during your activity. Some information may show up on the radio, on television, in nature, on signage as you drive... remain open to the many possibilities.

Many times negative thoughts come to mind during mind over matter practices. What do we do with that? We know that there is a concept out there that says think only good things or fail. But this message is merely part of a larger effective practice. Burying negative thoughts for fear they would grow larger actually feeds negative growth. We may consciously forget about experiences (causes), but they manifest in the physical until we come to terms with them (effects).

I have found the Emotional Freedom Technique to be extremely helpful to acknowledge a problem and then release it. I have a training video online (go to Youtube and type keywords "Michelle Payton EFT") that you can review at no cost and you can also find a training chapter on this technique in my book *Healing What's Real*. Basically what you do is tap on certain pressure points, which are called meridians, to release emotional pressure. It's been described as acupuncture without the needles. The theory is everything is tied into emotions, and non-physical and physical ailments are released through this technique very quickly.

Another interesting exercise that I've done to evaluate my perceived shortcomings or negative thoughts is to write down my top 5 negative thoughts about myself then step back from them. Some people burn these ideas after writing them to do a symbolic release. That's worked. I could EFT Tap on these personal disappointments. That's worked. But I decided to test another concept and keep the written information and see how stepping back from them and keeping them for review created improvement over time. No wordsmithing. I just wrote out my pure disappointment.

What took over with this exercise was synchronicity. Of course, to realize that synchronicity has occurred, you have to pay attention. When you pay attention, you consciously receive the information and take action. For instance, I was very disappointed in myself for not having a yoga classroom experience for nearly a year at one point. I practice yoga stretching and deep breathing daily, but the classroom experience is a full hour plus of listening, following, learning and joining energy of other like minded individuals.

Not more than a week later, one of my favorite yoga teachers said she was having a yoga class reunion of sorts and asked me to come. I did attend and it became my favorite weekly class.

I know. It seems like a complete contradiction to what I've said in other passages in this book. That's what's cool about it. There are so many ideas. Decide what fits for you. Keep an open mind when new ideas show up.

Financial Freedom with Less Money and Disciplined Follow-Through

He is able who thinks he is able.   —Buddha

When I wrote my book *"Soul"utions* I included thoughts on panicking about not having enough money. I owned an international distribution company where people counted on me to send them checks every month as well as doing my own work as an author, empatherapist, mind over matter practitioner and teacher. I loved what I did, but I wondered if I needed to re-think where I was dedicating my time.

Around the time of the September 11th attacks to the US, small businesses were feeling a moderate pinch. Businesses assumed that economic history would repeat itself and spending would readjust in a year or so and all would be well. But as the next eight years ticked away, many small businesses were experiencing flat to decreased sales year upon year. By 2009, the housing market collapsed, unemployment hit all time highs, and the government was bailing out banks, insurance companies, car manufacturers and more to keep US citizens from experiencing another Great Depression.

But here is what was really interesting. A couple of years prior, I seeded thoughts (by writing and posting these plans where I could regularly see them) on being at zero balance on my credit cards and business loans, and that when we sold our home in Ohio, we would get a loan for 5% or less. It was idealistic, but I let it simmer with the Universe and with my psyche or subconscious.

For the zero balance on business loans and all credit cards, when I wrote it I added a "by when" of December of that year. The first year passed and it didn't happen. The next year I made even less money than the year before with my company, but I held my plan in place for the consecutive December. That December came and went—balances had fallen, but never to zero. The next year I made even less money, but I was consistently paying business balances down, I was spending less personally and professionally where possible, and where I couldn't spend less I was making sure that I was working with my accountant to clearly log expenses in places where I got legal tax credits. I identified missed opportunities like, on a personal note, for years my husband and I delivered Meals on Wheels and items to the Free Store and never logged the mileage write off. That was a major lost opportunity as we would drive up to 75 miles a month.

The idea of living more simply became a stronger pull. After several years, my patterns changed on where I really needed to spend money. I was clearing things out my home and office constantly to keep the energy moving and the chi dancing through all physical areas. My follow-through also included as large as possible monthly credit card payments while still being able to realistically pay cash for monthly expenses (for work and personal). If cash ran out in a particular month for dinners out, clothing, entertainment…, so did the spending. While financial advisors were not big on this idea, we did some refinancing of debt for my sole proprietor business using our home as collateral. Again, not following financial advisors, I cashed in 10% of my IRA retirement to stabilize my company (paid big penalties later but remained on a cash basis). And when we sold our Ohio home and moved to North Carolina, we purchased a less expensive home with a much lower (unheard of) interest rate (Guess what? 5%!). And while my company billings were not as high as they'd been in past years, my credit cards and business loans were closing in on zero balance.

The simplicity created relaxation in my life. It made decisions on needs versus wants clearer. In connection to community, my signature continued to be received as honorable due to maintaining focus. And bonus, my children were picking up on patterns that would create life success for themselves as adults.

How are you living by example for yourself as much as for others? How simple can you make your life at this moment?

But I Can Help You! Hands-Off Follow-Through

It is better to conquer yourself than to win a thousand battles. Then the victory is yours. It cannot be taken from you, not by angels or by demons, heaven or hell.   —Buddha

It's the little things that can create complications then chaos. One day I was out shopping with my daughter, and we were stopped in our tracks as we were getting ready to go down an escalator. A high school aged young woman looked back at me and said, "It may take me some time to get on the escalator, I have been afraid of these since I was little."

I gave an "I understand" smile and looked at my own daughter and she said, "Mom, don't do it!" I responded, "But I can help her right now! She would never be trapped by this problem again. It would only take me a few minutes." "Mom, no," she insisted. And we continued down the escalator.

I mentioned earlier that there is a technique that I use called Emotional

Freedom Technique™ (EFT™) for this and other types of phobias. It is a mind over matter technique that involves tapping meridians (dense nerve points on your face, upper body and hands) to release emotional tension which includes phobias like the one just mentioned. It would have taken just a few minutes to help her release the emotional connection to transporting herself on escalators. Minutes!

I talked to my husband the next morning and asked "Should I have, in the middle of the mall, given a more mainstream explanation that the brain connects with certain tapping points, like acupuncture without needles, to release the emotional connection to a phobia?" Was my daughter supposed to see this in action to realize that the mind over matter techniques that I work with are effective, but I bailed due to fear of not being mainstream acceptable? Or was my daughter my teacher in regards to boundaries? My (more mainstream than metaphysical) husband's response was, "You don't know if she really wanted your help." But my thought kept going back to "Wouldn't someone trapped by this type of fear want help?" It's like watching someone choking on food, but being afraid to apply the Heimlich maneuver.

How can you give others information so that they can follow-through in ways they never knew possible? When is it appropriate?

The Art of Understanding Others Follow-Through

If you want others to be happy, practice compassion. If you want to be happy, practice compassion. —Dalai Lama

Maybe you've found yourself in this type of situation. I was in a discussion with someone who had opposing views. He became even more perturbed when I responded in a certain manner using certain words that he found unacceptable to his personality type.

I'll be clear that I am a major proponent for taking responsibility and ownership as a communicator. But another way to also increase positive interaction is to receive information as intended (even if it is clumsy or not as artful) from the sender.

For instance, when my husband was pickpocketed in Paris, I texted a number of my inner circle to let them know. The varied responses made me smile as it was truly a lesson in "embracing diversified personalities 101."

Some of the initial responses were:

"Oh, no. Are you with him? Is he ok? Please tell him I'm sorry." —An Aries with a pattern of liking to inspire

"...That guy will get his. Did he also get his social security card?" —A detailed Virgo with background in social work

"Paris, Ohio?" —An Aquarian with a relaxed personality

"What is this world coming to? ... My husband wears a money belt." —A Leo who is very organized and process oriented (husband who wears money belt is also a Leo)

"That sucks."—A Taurus who has gone through many hard knocks

One of the things I like most about studying personalities is that I get where they are coming from when I "receive" their responses. I'll be clear that it doesn't mean that I agree or like it. It just means that I understand how minds wrap around situations and that increases relaxation because less time is spent on missed understandings.

There are times when communicators take advantage of the fact that our minds click into a state of confusion. They do this, consciously or unconsciously, by recognizing mind patterns. Children are great at this. They know if they ask questions or permission when you are doing other things, it may be just chaotic enough to get the answers they want. We are basically in a light trancelike state creating an inability to consciously cope with so many situations or questions at one time. A looser term for this would be "playing with your mind."

At the end of the day, you can't change a person's mannerisms (what you perceive as rude, inconsiderate, disrespectful), only the way that you decide to receive them. I use Astrology, Numerology and Birth Order information as a baseline for understanding personalities (I've written three books in a series called *Birth Mix Patterns*), but if I don't have that basic information I look at (and this can change depending on the situation at hand):

- Is this person a pleaser or an aggressive leader?
- Is this person a talker or a listener?
- Is this person a researcher or intuitive?
- Is this person an introvert (loner) or extrovert (social)?
- Is this person an inward processor (thinks before talks) or outward processor (thinks out loud)?
- Does this person like to plan or go with the flow?
- Is this person the responsible one or prefers that others are responsible?

If you can answer only one of these questions through quick observation or even direct questions like "do you like to plan or go with the flow?" that can increase the effectiveness of your communication immensely. Getting to know just a bit about others, creates empathy and compassion and the very meaning of the compassion is love for humanity. We can all use a bit more of that in the world.

The Generation Gap and Sensitivity Training Follow-Through

*Whether one believes in a religion or not, and whether one believes
in rebirth or not, there isn't anyone who doesn't appreciate kindness and compassion.*   —Dalai Lama

It was a major learning curve to be a conduit to activating passion points
for my kids. What I did know is that kids (and adults for that matter)
will likely succeed sooner than later if they have a general direction. By
the time my son entered high school, I could see that he was drifting so I
regularly seeded ideas on what he might like to do when he was an adult.
My mother-in-law—laid back, nurturing, and about 30 years older than
I—felt it was too early to expect him to know where he was headed. Her
generation and experiences led her down the path that finding jobs and
making good lives was inherent. Part personality makeup and part age
difference, I disagreed as I watched unemployment and homelessness soar.
This is a good time to step back to describe generation gaps. According
to Pew Research (April 12, 2010). Here are the generations:

Generation "Y"/ Echo Boomers/Mellennials—born after 1980

According to Pew, this is the largest group of live births, during this
time period, in the history of the United States. They want it NOW,
value friends and family more than jobs, they work because they like it
not because it's required, and are informal.

Generation "X"—born around 1965 through 1980

This is a very independent group. Their first loyalty is to themselves
since they moved into the adult world of downsizing and cutbacks.
They look for meaningful experiences and challenges, and are savvy and
entrepreneurial.

Baby Boomers—born around 1946 through 1964

They came from the generation of financial security in the US. They can be self indulgent, move from one company to the next, are nostalgic yet anti-establishment.

Silent Generation—born around 1928 through 1945

These are children of the Great Depression and World War II. They had stable careers, worked for one or two companies in their professional lives, were non-risk takers and conformists.

So there is quite a contrast in each of these groups. My mother-in-law is from the Silent Generation, I am from the tail end of the Baby Boomers (1963), and my son is from Generation "Y."

In a Pew Survey, they asked each generation what makes theirs most unique (these were open-ended questions, and were responses given by those who said their generation was unique/distinct). They answered

Generation "Y"/ Echo Boomers/Millennials:

Technology Use (24%)

Music/Pop Culture (11%)

Liberal/Tolerant (7%)

Smarter (6%)

Clothes (5%)

Generation "X":

Technology Use (12%)

Work Ethic (11%)

Conservative/Traditional (7%)

Smarter (6%)

Respectful (5%)

Baby Boomers:

Work Ethic (17%)

Respectful (14%)

Value/Morals (8%)

"Baby Boomers" (6%)

Smarter (5%)

Your guess is as good as mine on why "Baby Boomer" was what made their generation unique. Maybe some consider this generation a type of brand name.

Silent Generation:

WWII/Depression (14%)

Smarter (13%)

Honest (12%)

Work Ethic (10%)

Value/Morals (10%)

"Work ethic" showed up in the top 5 uniqueness responses for all but Generation "Y"/Millennials. A job was less about identity and more about something that allows them to live life to its fullest—a true "Work to Live" approach.

OK. I've digressed a lot with statistics, but sharing generation trends also helps us mentor and parent with sensitivity on where people's heads are. So I/we (my husband and I) watched what our oldest daughter was good at—math and science, and she liked understanding how things worked, including the human body. At the time I was writing this book, she entered college to study nursing and was considering many different routes for graduate school and beyond, including being a doctor. But, to our relief, her undergraduate degree would, at least, get her a decent job.

It wasn't until my Gen. "Y" son was clearer on what he wanted to do as an adult that his high school classes made more sense to him. When his interest became identified as being an English teacher, he felt more connected to certain courses and his grades improved. When his interest became identified as being a psychologist, his grades in psychology and other humanities improved. We constantly brought his attention to what he seemed to enjoy. It didn't mean that was where he would end up, but he would at least feel like he was moving through life with purpose.

I've often said to my husband (both of us tail-end of baby boomers), that I have enough drive for both of us. And as our kids hit the college track, I repeated this to my older children as well. But they, ultimately, have to make the decisions on their own to truly succeed and be fulfilled (which is a stronger pull for Generation "Y").

But what price do we pay (as parents and guardians), to fund our next generations "fulfillment?" On one hand it was easier for me: I came from a low income family, and grants and scholarships were easy to get. The payoff to the masses, in theory, was this created a more educated America and brought people like me out of a state of poverty and into being a productive, tax paying contributor to society. I went to school full-time and received funding for tuition, books and some living expenses. To pay for other expenses (car, food, rent, insurance), I worked. But regardless of how much money you make today, to put $10,000 to $20,000 or more per year into your yearly household expenses to pay for schooling is a major financial hit for most families. While there's emotional satisfaction—pride, status, sense of duty—being a parent doesn't technically show a positive financial return on investment.

However, we have insisted that our kids also have some skin in the game. The arrangement is, we/parents pay for a set portion and the kids pay for a set portion of their undergraduate degrees. With the allotted money, they make decisions about going to a public or private university, living at home or on campus. They must also maintain a certain grade point average. These types of decisions help them with life skills, it increases their commitment to their higher education, and they have motivation to graduate within a reasonable time frame and get on with their adult lives.

While the high schools that we have experienced have many good qualities, most are a little behind in life and/or college planning because they wait until the beginning of the students' senior years to put together a résumé of achievements. Even better planning would be to require them to understand the value of the activities that they participate in at the beginning of their high school years, and build a stronger resume' for college or a job. Life skills should be integrated into the high school curriculum—personal finance, checking account management, lease or rental agreements, loan acquisition and management, building credit—prior to leaving high school. Kids today are going to become less and less tolerant of adults if they believe they are wasting their time.

Similar to understanding birth mix patterns, getting to know their language (somewhat), motivations and generational culture can help run a happier household. You won't always like it.

When did generation factors have an impact on your productivity as a parent, mentor, guardian, and/or professional? How can you use the information about these multiple generations to create a more positive now?

Saving Future Resources and Conservation Follow-Through

It is necessary to help others, not only in our prayers, but in our daily lives. If we find we cannot help others, the least we can do is to desist from harming them. —Dalai Lama

In the 1950's the Silent Generation created a sense of safety for themselves by creating bomb shelters that included fully stocked shelves with food, water and alternate power. Moving into the 60's, Baby Boomers and Generation X's relaxed and shelters disappeared, but the seeding of an idea remained—finding ways to create a sense of security.

The term "Y2K" was on everyone's lips in 1999. Prior to the clock striking 12:01 AM on January 1, 2000, there was a rush to purchase paper products (toilet paper, napkins, paper towels) and other items. Many computers were not programmed to register the year 2000, so surely they would all shut down and our way of life would be at risk. January 2000 came and went and the benefactors were computer programming and packaged goods companies, and the idea of safety, security and independence lingered.

Plagued with tragedy in the early 2000's in America—attacks on American soil, hurricanes, floods, fires, gasoline prices, unemployment, challenging economic conditions where few industries are immune, oil spills—the drum beat was stronger.

By the year 2000, the US was extremely dependent on limited types of fuel. Much to the dismay of "old school" energy and automotive companies, part of the country's success would be based on its ability to diversify its energy sources. Tolerance for corporations' and countries' price gouging America was coming to an end. Finding tools for independence, individual American households began testing and running their vehicles on energy made from plants and other alternative fuels.

Similar to the 1990's when the computer chip shot the US economy into super power mode, exploring and successfully implementing additional types of fuels could help stimulate the next upturn in the US economy. For my own household, I've narrowed it down to a few things to maintain a certain standard of life. One of the simplest things (excluding computers, televisions and radios)—is basic refrigeration. For my peace of mind, in the least, you will find an external power generator in my garage in the event that we have power outages so I can preserve our food and have electricity for basic living.

To increase my personal energy independence and sense of security, one of the critical steps was to stop hoarding energy. The first thing I did was evaluate what my actual usage was in electricity by tracking my electric bills. Here is what I found with our approximately 4000 square foot heated former home in Kilowatts per month and 2600 square foot current home (for translation sake, 1000 Watts = 1 Kilowatt).

Per Month Usage in Kilowatts – 4000 Square Feet (Ohio Home)							
	2009 (6 mo.)	2008	2007	2006	2005	2004	2003
Ttl KW/yr.	6835	18723	22426	22742	22332	21591	19668
Avg KW/ month	1139	1560	1869	1895	1861	1799	1639
Avg KW/ day	38	52	62	63	62	60	55

Note: Gas Stove, Water Heater and Furnace. 2009 usage compared to same six months in 2008 was down by 26%.

Per Month Usage in Kilowatts – 2600 Square Feet (N.C. Home)		
	2009 W	2010 W
Ttl W/yr.	5036000	6411000
Ttl KW/yr.	5036	6411
Avg KW/month	1007	1069
Avg KW/day	34	36

Note: 2009 5 months measured. 2010 6 months measured. Gas Water Heater and Furnace. Electric Stove.

Once I found my baseline, I looked at common energy suckers in my household like:

- Hair blow dryers (twice the running rate of a refrigerator)
- Laundry dryers (electric up to 7 times as much as a refrigerator/gas about the same as a refrigerator)

- Flat irons or curling irons (twice the running rate of a refrigerator)

So then I went after the low hanging fruit and discontinued drying linens to save on the length of time I used my electric laundry dryer (basically towels and sheets). After they dry, I put them all in the dryer for a short period to fluff (so they look and smell better).

We ran our whole house fan and air ionizer twenty-four hours a day in Ohio (about 800 watts to run). While running the fan and ionizer can kill germs in the air and decrease dust, and our builder recommended we run them for various reasons, it was eating up a lot of energy. I turned the house fan to auto only (kicks in primarily when we need house heat or cooling), and I put smaller ionizer air filters that use a fraction of the wattage in key rooms instead.

Then I took a look at the energy sucking areas where we experienced standby, phantom, or vampire power. According to The Lawrence Berkley National Laboratory, who has tested and created a table on its website www.standby.lbl.gov, what these terms mean is that even though you believe you are not using an appliance, if it remains plugged into an electrical outlet, it is still being fed a percentage of energy. Depending on the item it can be from one to ten watts. But the good news is you can reduce your phantom watt usage by up to 75%! Here are some things I did:

- I have an office out of my home and at the end of the day and weekends, I unplugged nearly everything in my office.
- When we weren't using the toaster, coffee maker, blender… in the kitchen, it was unplugged.
- Cell phone and video game chargers were unplugged as soon as items were charged.
- Energy saving smart strips were installed in our major video game playing, television viewing, computer usage areas

- Radios, treadmill, any other charger… all unplugged when not in use

I was pleasantly surprised. Once we were consistent on our execution as a family, we decreased out electric usage 43% in the first three months!!! You can see the results on the next table. Notice September 2008 is when we turned off our whole house fan and installed the smart strips. Then in 2009 I also tracked if this was an actual electric company reading or estimate. You can see that our usage for October, November, December 2007 was 43% less! January through June 2009 vs. 2008 same time period usage was down 26% (6835 vs. 9235 KW for six months).

Per Month Usage in Watts (E=Estimate in current yr)				
		2009 W	**2008 W**	**2007 W**
Jan	E	1358000	1521000	1084000
Feb	A	702000	1390000	1191000
Mar	A	957000	1457000	1467000
Apr	A	956000	1503000	2572000
May	A	1106000	1313000	529000
Jun	A	1716000	2051000	2702000
Jul			2392000	2723000
Aug			2081000	2261000
Sep++			1946000	2535000
Oct			907000	1893000
Nov			964000	1937000
Dec			1198000	1532000
Ttl W/yr.		6835000	18723000	22426000
Ttl KW/yr.		6835	18723	22426
Avg KW/day		38	52	62

++September 29, 2008 turned off whole house fan, stopped drying towels with electric dryer and installed power strips.

It was so freeing when I understood our energy usage. And it is gratifying to know that enough information was out there to help me understand how to conserve, take good care of my family in the event that our external generator is needed and/or limitations are mandated on energy usage. I train my family everyday by example so they only use what is truly needed.

Websites come and go, but at the time of writing this book, www. heartland-rec.com/energy_use_calculator.htm has an online calculator for your monthly energy costs (you can search for others on the Internet). If you're detailed, you'll find this very cool!

In the following table I've listed top line estimates on wattage usage and costs of household appliances to help you evaluate then follow-through on your plan to live more energy independently. I found this at www.callawayelectric.com/Safety%20Tips%20Frames/average_cost.html. I am a bit more of a top line gal, but this was still easy enough for me to follow, not to mention a huge eye opener.

Note that certain appliances need a different level of energy to start vs. maintain usage. This is not listed below, but this is very important to know when using an external generator (a wattage reference guide is provided when purchasing). For instance, a refrigerator/freezer has a running wattage of approximately 700 watts, but needs additional starting watts of 2200. Below are solid averages.

Appliance	Typical Wattage	Comment
Blender	386*	
Blow Dryer	1200	
Box Fan	200	
Bread Maker	675	
Broiler - Portable	1436*	
Can Opener	100	
Carving Knife	92	
CD Player	10	
Central Vacuum	1440	
Clothes Dryer	5500	
Coffee Maker	894	
Computer	450	

Curling Iron	30	(other sources quote 1500)
Deep Fryer	1448*	
Dehumidifier	390	
Dishwasher	1201	
DSS Satellite Receiver	24	
Edger	190	
Electric Blanket	177*	
Electric Grill	1580	
Electric Smoker	1500	
Fax Machine	105	
Food Freezer - Manual Defrost		
14 cu.ft.	695	
18 cu.ft.	580	
20 cu.ft.	600	
24 cu.ft.	640	
Food Freezer - Frostless		
14 cu.ft.	695	
18 cu.ft.	750	
20 cu.ft.	790	
24 cu.ft.	845	
Frying Pan	1196*	
Garage Door Opener	800	
Garbage Disposal	700	
Hair Rollers	350	
Heat Lamp - Infrared	250	
Heater - Portable	1500*	
Heating Pad	65*	
Hedge Trimmer	265	
Hot Plate	1257*	
Humidifier - Tabletop	177	
Ink Jet Printer	150	
Iron	1008*	
Laser Printer	350	
Lawnmower - Electric	561	
Lawnmower Cordless	40	(Charge only—20 hour charge = 1 mowing time)
Microwave Oven	1450	
Mixer	127	
Popcorn Popper	575	
Range w/Oven	12000	
Range w/Self-Cleaning Oven	13700	
Razor - Electric	14	
Refrigerator/Freezer-Manual		
14 cu.ft.	585	
18 cu.ft.	630	
20 cu.ft.	650	

Refrigerator/Freezer - Frostless

14 cu.ft.	670
18 cu.ft.	720
20 cu.ft.	780
24 cu.ft.	810
Roaster	1333
Sewing Machine	175
Stereo	16
Television**	110
Toaster	1146
Trash Compactor	800
Vacuum Cleaner	1300
Vaporizer	480
VCR	25
Video Game Unit	17
Waffle Iron	1116
Wall Clock	4
Washing Machine	512
Water Bed	350 – 500
Water Heater	4500
Weed Eater	300
Whole House Fan	370

**Instant-on televisions consume 75% of total wattage when not in use.
*Appliance operated at maximum range.

These computations are based on local data or information provided by the Electrical Energy Association.

For some, leaving a smaller carbon footprint is a goal. Maybe others are concerned about global warming. I would make the argument that this is as much about being a responsible consumer and community leader in your own household. But if you relate to none of these ideas, it does save you money.

What plug can you pull right now to decrease phantom watts from impacting your pocketbook? How does it make you feel when you are energy independent?

Integrative Energy and
Middle Class Follow-Through

To be idle is a short road to death and to be diligent is a way of life; foolish people are idle, wise people are diligent. —Buddha

I've noticed that there is a general belief that if you live in a middle class neighborhood, then you are believed to be conservative. One of the reasons why there may be a conservative perception is that some of the middle class may seem to be more calculating when it comes to how they spend their money. Some of those reasons could be that this "group" we'll call it, doesn't qualify for grants to fund college for their kids so the money comes from their savings or loans. Nor do they get the tax shelters of the wealthy, so what they have accumulated is dependent on the professional positions they hold at the moment (generally speaking).

But because there is some financial independence with the middle class, it's important to differentiate between the concepts of calculated risk and community responsibility. For instance, in this same income cluster, we should be seeing more leadership with solar power and other integrative energy resources. We can measure that traditional energy resources have become more limited therefore are increasing in cost. We can't measure as accurately (at the moment) how many households can decrease the demand on one energy resource so the price drops and there is a healthier return-on-investment. In economic terms, while the law of "Supply and Demand" would apply to part of the equation, there is no dollar figure that can be assigned to community responsibility or leadership.

After decreasing our home electricity usage by nearly 40% in some cases, we had a handle on how much energy we used daily and could plan out what other energy generation tools we could use in our home and costs associated with that (especially since there was more sun in North Carolina than Ohio). What became frustrating about this was the housing association's adverse reaction to seeing the panels on our roof. Basically the rule was "as long as we can't see the panels, it's ok." While with my home, I could abide by most of the rules, a large number of the homes in our area could not. It takes more than one house to create a revolution!

The area in Ohio I came from was also integrative energy adverse in a more subtle way. They didn't want to see clothes lines in yards to dry clothes to save energy. And I was even breaking the housing association laws by having a vegetable garden with a discreet fence in my back yard.

I get that housing associations are the suburban answer to zoning and protecting home values, but at any income level, we as a country have to be smarter when using energy sources. This requires that we reframe what we see as beautiful.

My husband and I were blessed with a free trip from his company to Hawaii (Oahu) and as we saw beautiful greenery, beaches, waterfalls, and sunsets, we also saw solar panels on the roofs of many houses. It was a beautiful sight to see the locals committed to integrating solar energy into their lives.

Around the turn of the 21st Century, on the Northeast coast, wind turbines were being added to the coastal landscape. A famous, wealthy family on that coast complained because it would ruin the view from one of the sides of their home. And they were known to be liberal Democrats! In contrast, my hometown (the mountains of North Carolina), there are visual plus nature preservation dilemmas, for example, how many trees would need to be cut down to accommodate wind turbines. What to do?

But more prominent companies are rising to the sustainability challenge. The Hilton (hotel) in Asheville (North Carolina) is "Green Building" certified, saving energy, creating water efficiencies, reducing CO_2 emissions, improving indoor environmental quality, showing sensitivity to use of overall resources and their impacts.

The Hilton installed a solar hot water system to heat the water throughout the hotel (including the pool), and has low flow toilets, showerheads and sink fixtures. They use "Energy Star®" light bulbs that last 10 times longer than traditional incandescent bulbs. They have a linen reuse program, a recycling program for guests and employees, and their restaurants donate its waste cooking oil to be recycled to bio fuel and more (keyword search on the internet "Hilton Asheville North Carolina" and click on their sustainability program button).

We may not change the "not in my backyard" tendency of many of the middle and upper class, but we can help redefine beauty resulting in preserving our environment. A number of interesting integrative energy studies are introducing the possibility of small cities like Asheville (NC) being nearly energy independent by using solar power in the summer and wind turbines in the winter. There is a delicate balance. I am excited by the possibilities, and am in the planning stages of reducing our household carbon emissions with ideas like solar power.

If you have the funding, can you consider solar, wind power, or other diversified energies? What can you do right now to only use the power that you truly need?

Understanding the Universal Language and World Peace Follow-Through

Where ignorance is our master, there is no possibility of real peace. —Dalai Lama

Speaking of the pocketbook, everyone wants world peace. OK, well many want world peace. And some believe world peace is achieved through a united world religion as long as you believe in "my God" and follow "my leaders." In contrast, there is the "All Are One" theory. It's like the "world think tank." We don't necessarily embrace one another's daily practices, but we are all plugged into one soul source. (Call this whatever feels right to you.)

Is world peace about spirituality? It can be or it doesn't need to be. What is the physical expression of "All Are One?" How does it connect to the wellbeing of our collective world? This may not be popular, but I'll drop the bomb as it were.

Walk into medium to large corporations anywhere in the world and there is a reconnect to the all are one concept. In a large percentage of countries, English is the first business language. For instance, I worked for a European company for a number of years, and to be in middle management or above you were required to do business in English. So we have a language in business to unite world commerce. And smart investors of all levels diversify their portfolios, committing a certain percentage of their money all over the world. So aware or not, like it or not, commerce unites the world. Unlike the Great Depression in the US (1929-1939), it's even clearer today that multiple countries were concerned about America's financial demise in 2008 and forward because they have major investments in the States.

I know. I know. Buy American and local! I like the idea of buying and selling American (Canadians like the idea of buying Canadian, and so forth), but there are times when buying overseas or over the border is attractive. Look at fair trade, tea, and New Age spirituality products and practices. As controversial as it may be, there are some jobs that are sourced overseas by American companies that the US really won't benefit by having on our soil (wow, I am not being popular here) or because the professionals are simply smarter (India comes to mind for computer technology). A weak world economy, no matter how you slice it, creates negative energy. Conscious and Unconscious investors protecting their interests will create world peace because their survival also depends on economically thriving. Sounds shallow I know, but money is a global energy exchange and it is part of our path to creating world peace!

But it's not just about corporations. My husband decided to spend an extra day (following his business meetings) in Paris for pleasure. He took a morning stroll to get a coffee and a woman jumped in front of him and said in English, "Look, I just found a ring. Do you think it's gold?" He replied in English, "It looks like it." And she looked inside the ring and showed him, "Yes, look, it is!" My husband thought nothing of this (except, well good for her) and went on his way. Then he was sitting on a bench drinking his coffee (texting me via cell phone) in front of the Louvre when another woman popped up next to him and said in English, "Look, I just found a ring. Do you think it's gold?" He thought it odd for this to happen again. What are the chances? But again, thought little of it, got up to look at the subway map, while also holding maps in his hands. It became clear that he was not only a tourist, but an American with no mastery of the language when a young man began speaking to him in French. My husband's French was weak and he spent a little too much time being cordial and the young Frenchman had just enough time to steal his wallet and run off down the subway. Within minutes my husband texted me again, "Can you call me right away? I just got pickpocketed." So even at the most basic levels, while this wasn't quite so positive, money is the one exchange that everyone wants and understands.

How does it feel to embrace the idea that the world is your backyard? If money is not an exchange of energy, then what is it? If money is not a form of Universal language, then what is?

Clearing Negativity with Energy Management Follow-Through

Faith is not something to grasp, it is a state to grow into.
                              —Mohandas Gandhi

So returning to your backyard, as I've space cleared homes and offices over the years, there are a number of reasons why energy gets stuck. I do this to my own home a number of times a year depending on what has transpired in my and my family's lives.

Before I go on with my personal story, I'll explain this so you understand how you can easily do this on your own as well. The shorter version of my space clearing process—to get energy to flow through your entire space evenly—equates to making sure that all your blood is flowing equally through your body and internal organs are all working together. First, I have some dowsing rods (hold them loosely in my hands and let the subconscious take over) that I use to visually show me where energy is stuck. I ask my subconscious—because when I get out of my own way consciously my subconscious taps into the Universal knowledge—"please show me where the energy is stuck or negative." I walk through the space and the rods cross where I need to focus extra attention. Obvious areas are where there is clutter, corners of rooms, closets, and unused rooms. Less obvious is everywhere else (I know, that really narrows it down).

Then I "smoke it out." This means I burn herbs in a flat shell and fan the smoke through the area with a feather (feather is not required). I keep my intentions positive to clear the area so that all that remains is loving, kind, nurturing energy. Now and again I may talk to my spiritual sources, higher self... to ask for extra help.

Regarding herbs, I grow my own space clearing herbs, for the most part, and what I don't grow I can buy locally. Buying locally is good for many reasons—fewer hands touch the herbs and you know they are relatively fresh. Any herb that has been dried for longer than a year, I give back to the Earth (by composting it). Generally speaking, herbs dried after one year, have lost their life force. I will usually use anything from just sage to a combination of sage, rosemary and lavender. Composting can be as simple as throwing it in your existing garden to throwing it in the woods that may be on your property, or burying it in the ground.

After I smoke out the area I check the energy levels again with my dowsing rods. If the rods are still crossing in certain areas—my sign for energy needing to be reframed to being positive and supportive—then I go back and smoke it out until the rods indicate that all is clear.

Then my last step is to spray my version of holy water in the area. I have picked up sacred water in a number of areas of the world, and just use a few drops to combine with clean water (could be boiled or another type of filtered or sterilized water). I will add essential oil like lavender (a natural antiseptic as well as it smells good and is calming). Sometimes I put water outside to soak up the sun and moonlight (especially if it's a unique moon) before I use it. There are many philosophies and processes, but I always use some type of blessed water to finish out my ceremony.

With the longer version, I will drum out the area first or clap (the hands can get pretty sore depending on the size of the space). This means that I make all kinds of noise by beating a drum throughout the area. Especially corners, closets, basements and storage areas. This encourages the energy to move more freely. While I use dowsing rods to check my work, others may use bells. They hit the chime or bell and it stops ringing more abruptly than areas that are clear.

Once the space is cleared, I look for the heart center of the home by using my dowsing rods (I equate this to the human heart center... the heart pumps the blood or energy throughout the entire vessel). In this space I set up a discreet altar, symbol or simply sit in the space and program (some may call this praying) the healthy intention into the space. It should be clutter free to flow well.

As a reminder, this is a process in which I've combined many concepts that feel right to me. And it's all about intention.

OK. So on to my story. Once we arrived in North Carolina and I finally had all the boxes unpacked, I pulled out my space clearing kit. We had a company move all of our belongings from Ohio to North Carolina and many people touched our things, plus it all sat in a truck for days. On top of that, the energy with my family was a combination of confused on what their routines should be, loneliness for old friends, missing our oldest daughter, and anger for being forced to move, among other things. My son had a really bad first couple of days when we moved to North Carolina so I expected some negative activity, but when I checked his room I was alarmed when I was dowse checking. I had never energetically checked a space so packed with unsupportive energy. When I went into my eight-year-old's room her bed was also an energy stopper, however, intuitively I sensed that this was because she had some tough interactions with little friends at times in our former home and this energy was absorbed. But what really threw me off was the negative energy in my oldest daughter's room (that hadn't made it to North Carolina yet) and the futon in our guest room. My son had friends that visited (from our former home) and slept in these areas, but instead of investigating I quickly got to the clearing work to the point of setting off our smoke alarms (my kids never let me live that one down).

In contrast, when checking the first floor and our master bedroom there were only a few stuck places and they were there because of low use and energy slumping in corners.

When I talked to my son about my space clearing experience, he said, "There was a lot of anger processing going on in my room so that makes sense." And one of his friends, that was still visiting, said that he and the other guest/friend got into a couple of huge arguments while staying in our home and that would likely be a contributor to the energy issues in those rooms. It's always interesting to hear the physical stories in connection to energy work.

On the mainstream end of the spectrum, my family is regularly concerned when I space clear that when we have visitors the sage and other herbs may be mistaken for heavy partying at the Payton household. It does the trick and keeps the chi in our home dancing happily through our space afterwards, but I usually space clear at night so that it's less obvious. I was even more sensitive to the aromas when I was selling my house in Ohio, because I found myself doing quick space clearings when I had a lot of potential buyer traffic. Clearing unknown visitor comments from our space kept our family from absorbing unsupportive energy.

If you feel like you need support, let your environment be one for the first things you freshen up. Keep simple things on hand like sage to get the clearing ball rolling, then expand from there.

Clearing Nervous Jitters and Emotional Management Follow-Through

The mind is everything. What you think you become.

—Buddha

So now you can clear your space, but how many times have you needed to clear yourself?

When my third grader started a new school, she also started soccer for the first time (she begged for this even though she hates sweating and running), and horseback riding lessons. We also moved into a new house, a new state, and found new friends. By the first full week of school, my youngest was a bundle of nerves. She liked school, but she was having separation anxiety, missed her old friends, and was experiencing fatigue with so many new things in her life. So when her teacher called me the second week of school and said she had her head on her desk complaining of a tummy ache and crying for me, I knew it was time to kick into "mind over matter mom."

I suggested (or anchored in my youngest's mind) when picking her up at school that the reason why her tummy was upset was likely that her body was adjusting to her new experiences, not going to bed early enough, and not drinking enough water (so I could keep her immune system strong while we worked through other issues). I suggested that while I know she missed her daddy, me, her summer routine, and her former home and friends, she could move past those emotions if, for starters, we paid closer attention to getting to bed earlier, drinking more water, and being open to new friends and experiences.

So we agreed to a time for her to be in bed. It didn't mean she had to sleep immediately, but that she was preparing to sleep. And we agreed that sipping water throughout the day would also be helpful (versus gulping too much at one time). We also did a session of Emotional Freedom Technique™ tapping. We tapped on ideas like:

Even though I miss mommy and daddy, I'm happy to be in school; Even though I'm scared at school sometimes, I'm ready to learn, listen and have fun at school; Even though my tummy hurts at school, I feel better as soon as I hear my teacher giving me instructions (anchoring her teacher's voice with feeling better); Even though my tummy is upset at school, I'm ready to listen and learn and get good grades at school (I thought I may as well slip this in).

I could have been very basic and said "Even though my tummy hurts, I love myself." But (for me) telling a story and suggesting to the subconscious additional positive ideas is like getting EFT bonus points while still remaining vague enough to have the brain interpret the information to serve its higher good. It reminds me of the movie "Men In Black" with Will Smith. He and his partner had this mind suggestion tool that when people looked into it he could erase their memories, but he could also make suggestions like "Get a job. Change your wardrobe. Clean your house." EFT doesn't erase memories, but taps into the subconscious mind to remove negative emotional attachments which ultimately protects the physical body from adverse absorption and reaction.

As the next week wore on, she was still having stomach aches saying, "Mom, I don't care if we tapped! My stomach still hurts!" What that said to me is that we didn't tap out the issues completely. She had, what I call as a mainstream metaphysical mom, emotional stomach (not a medical term). To add to her turmoil, this daughter is a Pisces and Life Path 11 (see my *Birth Mix Patterns* books for more information), so she is a cosmic psychic sponge picking up on others' energies. So I reminded my daughter of her pressure points for stomach soothing, gave her another pressure point to decrease anxiety/increase comfort, and reminded her to take 3 to 5 deep breaths to increase comfort. In addition, I contacted her teacher for continuity so when her emotional stomach kicked in, she could advise her to use her pressure points and deep breathing for relaxation. Finally, our daughter was in a more comfortable space and when we dropped her off in her classroom she had a smile on her face (most of the time).

When do you find yourself getting nervous? What if you had a technique to calm your nerves? To see more about the Emotional Freedom Technique you can go to YouTube and in the keyword search type "Michelle Payton EFT."

Lessons During My Haircut Nine Years After 9/11 and Finding Teachers Follow-Through

The way is not in the sky. The way is in the heart. —Buddha

There are times when shock is the only thing you can feel. If you read the first book in the *Adventures of a Mainstream Metaphysical Mom* series, you would have seen my story on where I was and what I was doing at the moment of impact on the fated day of September 11, 2001 in America. It was a surreal day, like I was watching a movie vs. a newscast.

Nine years later (nearly to the day), my teenage son said, "I hate going to school on September 11th. There's always some group that is making a big deal and being depressing." I thought this was an interesting comment from my son because he was 8-years-old (in third grade), when this happened. As he headed into adulthood and heard anything about September 11th, he would have likely blocked it out of his mind because of the way people have communicated it as he was growing up. That was until this day.

It just so happened that our hair designer was doing his fine work (cutting my hair) when he told us that he lived in New York City when the towers were hit. He watched the towers burn from the roof of his apartment. And when he went onto the street he said he'd always remember the faces covered with soot and all he could see were the whites of people's eyes. It was beyond words when he saw the towers collapse. Prior to 9/11, when NYC had their blackout, he said that there was terrible looting and crime. But post 9/11 black out, the people of New York came together, pulled their frozen meat out of their freezers and had big cookouts and shared with their neighbors and friends.

The reason why we were lucky enough to have him as our family hair designer (in North Carolina) is he never again wanted to go through the absolute isolation that New Yorkers experienced during those emergencies. It was nearly impossible to get off the island during these disasters and with all the climate changes and NYC sitting on a fault line with buildings that weren't designed to withstand earthquakes (similar to LA and San Francisco), he decided to move. (Note that this is one person's path. New York City is an amazing place with much to offer for many.)

This is an American experience reframe that I could have never taught my son. But here we were, getting our monthly haircuts, hearing this gripping story from someone we knew, liked and trusted.

When were you just doing your daily "stuff" when all of a sudden your reality was rearranged? Our lessons come from the most unlikely teachers. Be alert so you can take advantage of every one of them.

Who Do You "Talk" to and Higher Self Follow-Through

We can live without religion and meditation, but we cannot survive without human affection. —Dalai Lama

When we land in crisis situations, many look to a higher source. That means many things to many people and they explore in many different ways. I believe this is why all the magical stories like *Harry Potter*, the *Twilight* series, Ghost and Psychic television shows and movies have become so popular in the 2000's.

For instance, I enjoy "ghost hunter" type shows. We record them and then we devour a few hours at a time when we can carve out the time. By "we" I mean my youngest daughter and me (and my oldest when she is home from college). My husband and son make fun of us (but heads turn when something really eerie shows up) as we "ooh" and "ah" over the voice recordings and infrared detectors that show heat signatures, watch the video, and learn about theories like cold spots, intelligent hauntings and continuous reel type hauntings. We chit chat about the intuitive professionals, the history, the processes to bless a space to rid it of evil entities and to help souls cross over. With my youngest, who is elementary school aged, and being a Pisces and Life Path 11 (strong intuitive), it's a great bonding activity. And when viewing these supernatural experiences, discussions begin to evolve into "Who would I call on if I felt like I needed protection?"

I have a strong pull to what I call a Mother Father God (more androgynous representing both feminine and masculine energy). The primary reasons why many have called God "him" for thousands of years is classic (mostly male) artist renditions show God as male and because we are (for the most part) a patriarchal society using "he" as a default. I, personally, feel most comfortable connecting to Earth Religions, and have a discomfort with proclaiming my allegiance to any one entity—being forced to say "do you promise to raise your child… or do you promise to live your life in allegiance to…" Part of this is because so many people misinterpret intentions. For instance, I feel there is a sacred energy connected to a Jesus figure, and I also feel we are equals. Maybe our potential is not entirely tapped, but equals nonetheless. I believe Mother Father God experiences through us—the collective or Universal consciousness—therefore we are a summation of Mother Father God. So without all of us, the concept of God—All are One—could not exist. If you are following this thought process (not believing, simply understanding), we are perfect spirits experiencing being imperfectly human.

I was with my extended family (in-laws, my mother and sister, nieces and nephews) and we were discussing matters of spirit and one said, "I feel bad that you can't experience church like I do and how it makes me feel." Another said, "If I knew that there was no Jesus and no God, I don't know what I would do." We express our spirituality in many different ways and truth, like beauty, it is in the eye of the beholder. Realize that even those who feel a connection to only themselves, no religion per se, are celebrating their spirits within. When I teach and attend classes, when I go to community gatherings, when I am with my family, when I work with clients, when I feel I am helping others… these and more fill my spirit up. My daily lessons are a part of my soul sustenance, because love, compassion, and kindness are lessons "speaking to me" everywhere.

In the same breath, I will say that all should do what makes them comfortable. It's whatever gets people through their days. Belief and faith is most effective when they spread love, kindness and compassion to everyone. For thousands of years, history has continued to repeat that while individual choices are very important, limited definitions can result in unhappiness, hatred, wars, and death if we become too rigid and insist on a homogeneous society. So when I ask for assistance outside of the physical realm my intention is to talk to, meditate with, and/or pray to all that connects to my highest good and the good of others.

Who and what seen and unseen forces give you strength?

V. Ompossibilities

Believe nothing, no matter where you read it, or who said it, no matter if I have said it, unless it agrees with your own reason and your own common sense. —Buddha

Regardless of what is in black and white or who says it, information should resonate with you before you assimilate it. If I provided one pearl of wisdom or I've given you information that you feel the exact opposite on, this clarity allows you to stand in your power. As I bring this to a close, I find myself reflecting back to my childhood. And why I made the decisions that I've made as a wife and lover, mother, professional, daughter, sister, aunt, friend, philanthropist, mentor, acquaintance...

I wrote this in my blog www.mainstreammetaphysicalmom.com when I found out my estranged father had passed away. The biggest emotion that I felt was relief. Here is the beginning of the blog.

THE DEATH OF A SALESMAN EULOGY: AT PEACE WITH THE LEARNING THAT CAME FROM AN ABUSIVE CHILDHOOD

What if you had to write a eulogy for someone that did you harm? Could you connect

the successes in your life with your experiences? Who or what would you write about?

While on my quest to find out more about the paternal side of my family (where my American Indian heritage originated), I also strived to remain separate from my biological father. This is where I also discovered that my father had died.

I hadn't connected with my father in 30 years due to the extensive abuse he inflicted on my entire family—in the form of alcohol, drug, physical, mental, and sexual abuse. I kept my distance for the first years to lick my wounds and create a more functional and happier me. The following years were to protect my children from the sickness that manifests from being re-exposed to such dysfunctional patterns. As the Nobel Peace prize winner, Albert Einstein once said, "the definition of insanity is doing the same thing over and over again and expecting different results."

When I heard of his crossing, I decided to write a healing eulogy for my father who always put on a face of "all is well" while creating chaos—the ultimate salesman spin. Here are my thoughts.

Thank you dad for the Christmases that were best celebrated late in the day because you were passed out drunk under the Christmas tree. It taught me to see more clearly through my children's eyes during these important family holidays.

Thank you, dad, for being such a masterful liar. It taught me to coach my children to "tell" if ANYONE touched or directed them to take any action that they felt uncomfortable or confused with.

Thank you, dad, for having us run out of town on numerous occasions because of your "indiscretions." It taught me to find the silver lining in any situation and that, no matter how bad it got, we still had it better than many others.

Thank you, dad, for allowing us to live in poverty on numerous occasions, having no utilities (water, electric, gas) because your money went to "other women," drugs and alcohol. It taught me the value of a dollar, an education, family, being loyal in relationships, and the importance of clean and healthy living (inside and out).

Thank you, dad, for the experiences of the past as they have brought me to such a wonderful place today. I am stronger, wiser, and have so much gratitude for my life. Find peace. I have found mine.

End of blog.

I've spent a great deal of time talking about my family and children in particular as they are the future. And one of the reasons why my father became such a destructive force is because he had a terrible upbringing, with cruel siblings and parents that did horrendous jobs. As he spiraled out of control, he reproduced, and left a trail of victims until they chose to break the pattern.

It's not what has been done to us, but what we choose to do with those experiences. While there are lots of parents that make lots of mistakes (me included), and community and world experiences that have let us down, there is a point in adulthood where it's 100% our responsibility to pull ourselves up from our bootstraps.

Consider using this as a tool even if the person(s) is still living and/or the event(s) is/are still in motion. How can you turn negative experiences into powerful learning tools? Look forward to a happier and productive life. Jump, with both feet, into your power. I did.

Hatred does not cease by hatred, but only by love; this is the eternal rule. —Buddha

About the Author

To survive and thrive past a childhood household of anger, poverty, alcohol, drug, mental and physical abuse, and divorce, at an early age Michelle learned to read situations quickly. Figuring out how to manifest positive outcomes in the long-term, Michelle became fascinated with how people's minds worked. Her eclectic (mainstream and metaphysical) studies over the past 25 years revolve around making others more comfortable with themselves and others bringing her to the title "Empatherapist." She uniquely blends holistic and clinical studies to create clarity and confidence, feelings of safety, predictability, and trust, putting you more in control of your actions. This understanding also creates compassion for others, and by definition, manifests a love for humanity and soul-based happiness.

She helps people to work from their heart centers as New Age parents, partners, professionals, and individuals with a Bachelor's degree in Communication Arts, as a Birth Mix Patterns™ Master and Creator (combining Astrology, Numerology, and Birth Order), as a Ph.D. and Doctorate (D.C.H.) in Clinical Hypnotherapy, as a Master (NLP) Neuro-Linguistic Programmer™, as a certified (EFT) Emotional Freedom Technique™ Practitioner, and as an Adodyne Imagery™Practitioner (for medical procedures), plus many other studies—Past Life Regression, Self Hypnosis, Reiki, Feng Shui… —to enhance her life and her clients' experiences.

She has touched people worldwide as an author, teacher, empatherapist, radio guest and as a writer for numerous regional and national publications. She offers empowering books, seminars and one-on-one sessions worldwide. She, her husband and life partner since 1982, and their three children reside in Asheville, North Carolina.

For more information on Michelle Payton's products and services visit:

www.TheLeftSide.com – for wholesale book purchases

www.MichellePayton.com – for retail purchases on books, seminars, and individual consultations

www.HelpingUExpand.com – for business and retail seminars and guest speakers in soul-based living

Phone: 828-681-1728

Emails: TheLeftSide@aol.com, MAMichellePayton@gmail.com

Mainstream and Metaphysical Living

from multiple award-winning author, Michelle A. Payton, Ph.D., D.C.H.

As a conscious living communicator and mind over matter professional, Michelle's work shares thoughts on how to accomplish 21st century, soul-based living as a mainstream and/or metaphysical parent, partner, professional, and individual, including how this has unfolded with her, her clients (with permission) and throughout history.

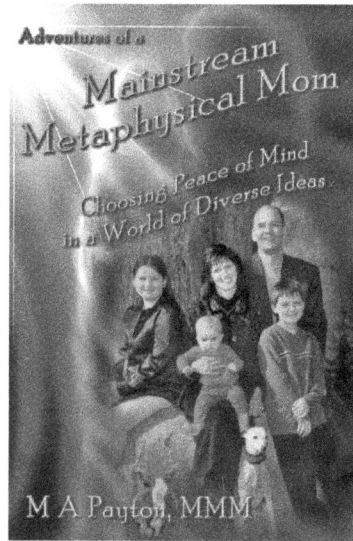

Adventures of a Mainstream Metaphysical Mom: Choosing Peace of Mind in a World of Diverse Ideas (Book 1)

Mainstream metaphysical parenting, mentoring, and relationships with self and others in the 21st century!

2003 Finalist for Best Biographical/ Self-Help Book

--Coalition of Visionary Resources, 2003 Visionary Awards, International New Age Trade Show

192 pp ~ paperback

ISBN 978-0-9719804-0-2

$13.95

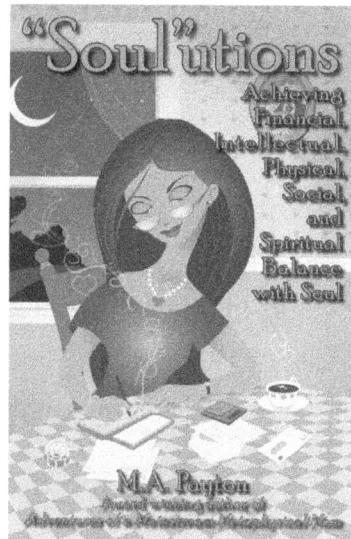

"Soul"utions: Achieving Financial, Intellectual, Physical, Social, and Spiritual Balance with Soul

Tips on soul-based living using goal setting principles in all areas of life!

239 pp ~ paperback

ISBN 978-0-9719804-1-9

$14.95

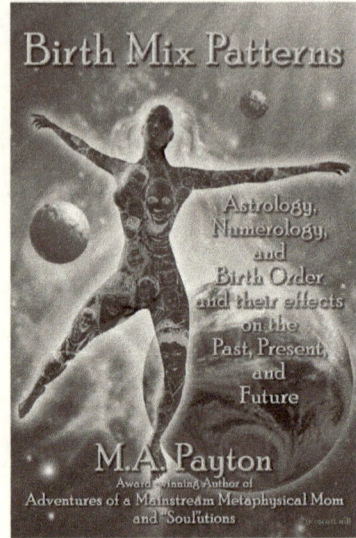

Birth Mix Patterns™: Astrology, Numerology, and Birth Order, and their Effects on the Past, Present, and Future

Analyzes hundreds of historical figures, including United States Presidents and First Ladies, artists, authors, civil rights leaders, and more in connection with astrology, numerology, and birth order.

2006 Finalist for Best General Interest/How To Book

—Coalition of Visionary Resources, 2006 Visionary Awards, International New Age Trade Show

160 pp ~ paperback

ISBN: 978-0-9719804-2-6

$12.95

Birth Mix Patterns™: Astrology, Numerology, and Birth Order, and their Effects on the Families & Other Groups that Matter

Analyzes the authors of the Declaration of Independence, dark leaders, the US Supreme Court Justices, the Beatles and more in connection with astrology, numerology, and birth order.

133 pp ~ paperback

ISBN 978-0-9719804-3-3

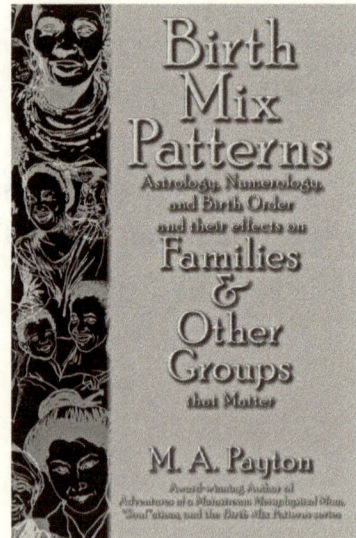

$12.95

Birth Mix Patterns™ and Loving Relationships using Astrology, Numerology, and Birth Order

Analyzes more than two dozen famous couples from Hollywood, to community servers, to same gender partnerships in connection with astrology, numerology, and birth order.

137 pp ~ paperback

ISBN 978-0-9719804-4-0

$12.95

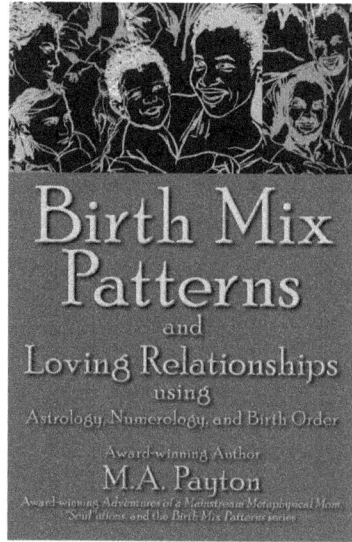

Healing What's Real: Expanding Your Personal Power with Mind Over Matter Techniques

Dr. Payton shares her experiences with Hypnotherapy, Neuro-Linguistic Programming™ (NLP), Emotional Freedom Technique™ (EFT), meditation, and more with dozens of transcribed sessions and interviews combining these techniques.

253 pp ~ paperback

ISBN 978-0-9719804-5-7

$15.95